LEGAL ANALYSIS

THE FUNDAMENTAL SKILL

LEGAL ANALYSIS

THE FUNDAMENTAL SKILL

SECOND EDITION

David S. Romantz
&
Kathleen Elliott Vinson

CAROLINA ACADEMIC PRESS
Durham, North Carolina

Library of Congress Cataloging-in-Publication Data

Legal analysis : the fundamental skill / David S. Romantz & Kathleen
Elliott Vinson. -- 2nd ed.
    p. cm.
Includes index.
ISBN 978-1-59460-279-5 (alk. paper)
    1. Legal research--United States. 2. Law--United States--Methodol-
ogy. I. Vinson, Kathleen Elliott, 1969- II. Title.

KF240.R636 2009
340.072'073--dc22

                                        2009019315

Carolina Academic Press
700 Kent Street
Durham, North Carolina 27701
Telephone (919) 489-7486
Fax (919) 493-5668
www.cap-press.com

Printed in the United States of America

To my family, for their support, encouragement, and patience.

KV

To my family, friends, colleagues,
students, and especially to LHH.

DSR

Contents

Acknowledgments

We are grateful to the following people who read and commented on the various drafts of the manuscript: Joan Malmud, Geraldine Griffin, Bridget Warner, Kathy Weiland, Joseph McKinney, Lauren Siegel, and John Brittingham. Their thoughtful comments and suggestions were invaluable. We are deeply indebted to Linda Hayes, Administration Secretary, the University of Memphis School of Law, for her outstanding and tireless administrative support in the writing and editing of this book. We are grateful to Suffolk University Law School and the University of Memphis School of Law for their generous financial support. We are indebted to our students as well as our own former teachers. Finally, thanks to Linda and Keith at Carolina Academic Press for their support and infinite patience.

LEGAL ANALYSIS

THE FUNDAMENTAL SKILL

$3-17$

$21-30$

Chapter 1

$\mathit{Prac.}$

$\mathit{Ex.\ 4}$

The Foundations $0-34$
of Legal Analysis

OBJECTIVES

WHEN YOU FINISH THIS CHAPTER AND COMPLETE THE EXER-
CISES, YOU WILL BE ABLE TO

* UNDERSTAND THE ROLE OF STATUTES
* UNDERSTAND THE ROLE OF CASE LAW
* UNDERSTAND THE RELATIONSHIP BETWEEN THE COMMON
  LAW, PRECEDENT, AND *STARE DECISIS*
* DESCRIBE THE HIERARCHY OF COURT SYSTEMS
* UNDERSTAND JURISDICTION
* IDENTIFY DIFFERENT TYPES OF AUTHORITY

Lawyers serve as advocates for their clients. They are hired to represent people, partnerships, corporations, property, and estates on a wide variety of issues ranging from the mundane to the complex. Lawyers are required to analyze an ever-increasing body of law that includes cases, statutes, ordinances, rules, and regulations and to apply that law to an infinite variety of fact scenarios. But how do lawyers craft meaningful legal arguments when the body of law and facts are so large and ever-changing? How do lawyers argue before a court with conviction? Can lawyers anticipate how a court would likely rule in a given case? The answers to these questions lie in an understanding of the foundations of legal analysis.

This chapter introduces the foundations of legal analysis. The foundations of legal analysis are the set of principles that lawyers use to analyze the law, devise legal arguments, and predict legal outcomes. Understanding these rules and principles is a crucial step towards becoming an effective advocate.

The foundations of legal analysis do not require attorneys to know the law by heart. The body of jurisprudence is too large and always changing. The rules and principles of legal analysis, however, allow attorneys to fashion credible and persuasive arguments on almost any legal issue. The key is to understand how the lawmakers, typically courts and legislatures, make and change the law.

This chapter introduces two important sources of law—statutes and case law. It also discusses three seminal principles of case-law analysis: (i) common law; (ii) precedent; and (iii) *stare decisis*. In addition, this chapter discusses the structure of court systems, basic principles of jurisdiction, and the weight or significance of legal authority. Together, these concepts form the foundation of American jurisprudence. They serve as some of a lawyer's most powerful tools.

A. Statutes

Statutes are one source of law that lawyers use to analyze problems. Typically, students in their first year of law school spend the majority of their time reading and analyzing judicial opinions. As a result, they often fail to recognize the importance of statutes. A statute is an act of a legislature that, among other things, proscribes and governs conduct. It is a formal written enactment of the legislative body. Statutes are only one kind of enacted law. Other enacted law includes ordinances, or municipal law, and regulations, or law derived from administrative bodies.

Legislatures have the exclusive constitutional authority to enact statutes. The federal legislature, the United States Congress, enacts laws that affect every person or legal entity across the country. In addition, each state has its own legislature with authority to enact laws that regulate conduct within that state's borders. Congress and the various state legislatures are independent, separate lawmaking bodies. Most legislatures are bicameral. They consist of two chambers, a Senate and a House of Representatives or Assembly.

The process of enacting a federal statute involves several stages. First, a legislator introduces a bill in his or her chamber of the legislature. The bill is then referred to a committee consisting of members from that chamber. A committee can be either permanent, called a standing committee, or temporary, called a special or ad hoc committee. The legislature's committee structure is organized so that each committee considers only legislative ideas of the same or similar subject matter. For example, the House of Representatives' Committee on Agriculture considers bills that relate to farm policy and nutrition.

Once a bill is assigned to a committee, the committee reviews the bill and invites experts and other interested parties to testify on the impact of that legislation. More importantly, the committee debates each section of the proposed law and amends, or marks up, the bill. After careful consideration, the committee votes up or down on the bill. If the bill wins support from a majority of committee members, then the bill is reported out of committee to the full chamber. If the bill fails to win a majority, then the bill is deemed "dead in committee." When a bill survives a committee vote, the committee issues a report, including a revised version of the bill. That report recommends whether the full chamber should approve the bill. The full chamber then considers, debates, amends, and finally votes on the bill. If the bill passes in the originating chamber, it goes through a similar process in the opposite chamber. When both chambers pass an identical bill, the bill is then presented to the President. If the President signs the bill, it becomes law. If the President does not sign the bill within ten days, it still becomes law. If the President vetoes the bill, the bill goes back to the legislature. There, the veto may be overridden by a two-thirds vote in each chamber. Barring a congressional override, the bill could be re-drafted to incorporate the President's objections or shelved.

State legislatures largely echo the federal model. In every state the governor must sign a bill into law and reserves the right to veto an objectionable bill. Once enacted, each statute becomes an independent source of law. Federal statutes govern persons and entities throughout the United States, while the reach of state statutes usually ends at the state's borders. Once enacted, a statute remains fixed unless changed or abolished by the legislature or declared unconstitutional by a court of competent jurisdiction. While courts can and do interpret the meaning and application of a statute's terms, they cannot amend its language.

B. Case Law

Another source of law is case law. Case law is law derived from the opinions of courts. Case law consists of both the common law and judicial decisions that interpret statutes and other enacted law.

The Law

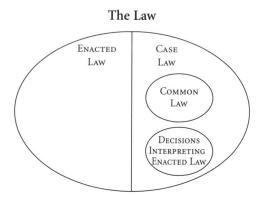

Courts make law in at least three ways.

First, a court may fashion a general legal doctrine or principle if it is required to resolve a case but no binding law exists to determine the matter. That new legal doctrine or principal is enforceable only within that court's geographic reach. By adopting or creating a new legal doctrine, a court creates binding law absent any legislative debate or vote. But, a court can create new law only in the absence of enacted law because enacted law trumps case law. For example, if neither the United States Congress nor a state legislature has enacted a law to protect victims of negligent infliction of emotional distress, a court may create a legal doctrine that recognizes the harm and provides a remedy to victims.

Second, a court also makes law by deciding cases that interpret existing legal doctrines. A court makes new law with each case it decides because each case comes before the court with a unique set of facts. When the court applies the law to a new set of facts, a new precedent is born that adds to the growing body of case law. An opinion that incorporates a new fact to an existing legal doctrine creates new law for the purpose of deciding future cases that include the same or materially similar facts.

Suppose a court decided that a plaintiff could recover for a defendant's negligent infliction of emotional distress. In that case, a defendant was liable to a mother when he accidentally shot and killed her young child in plain view of her mother. The court in that case limited its holding to allow only parents to recover, reasoning that the defendant knew or should have known that his negligent acts would harm a parent witnessing the shooting of her child. In a later decision, the court allowed a foster parent to recover under a similar set of facts. From that point forward, potential plaintiffs included all parents and foster parents. In a subsequent case, the court held that siblings were also included in the pool of potential plaintiffs. Each case added to or modified that state's case law by expanding the class of plaintiffs who could sue under a negligent infliction of emotional distress theory.

Third, courts make law by interpreting ambiguous or vague language in enacted law, such as statutes, ordinances, or administrative regulations. Sometimes, a legislature or other rule-making body will enact a law with terms that have more than one meaning or with terms whose meaning depends on context. Before a court can apply that law to the facts before it, it must construe the indefinite terms. The court's interpretation of ambiguous terms in enacted law determines how a later court should apply that law to similar cases in future disputes. Suppose a court interpreted a state statute regarding recycling. The relevant statute states that "all newsprint shall be collected and recycled." The issue before the court was whether magazines are considered newsprint. The court concluded that magazines were not newsprint for the purposes of the statute. In that case, the court added to the body of case law by construing an ambiguous term in a legislative enactment. That opinion now has the force of law on all similar cases.

Courts do not render decisions in a vacuum. Instead, courts abide by an important set of concepts to aid in their resolution of cases. Among these concepts are the common law, precedent, and *stare decisis*. In contrast to legislatively enacted statutory law, the common law consists of the rules and legal principles derived from judicial decisions rendered in the absence of enacted law. A precedent is any judicial decision or opinion that serves as an example of how a subsequent court can resolve a similar question of law under a similar set of facts. Finally, *stare decisis* is a time-honored maxim that requires courts to follow precedent when deciding similar cases.

1. Common Law and Precedent

Generally, the common law is case law rendered in the absence of enacted law. Under federal and state constitutions, only the legislature is empowered to make law. As such, courts can make law only to fill a void left by the legislature. The common law is derived from the body of judicial opinions.

A precedent is a judicial opinion that illustrates the application of legal rules and doctrines to the facts of a specific case. A precedent, if it examines a common-law rule, becomes part of the common law. Thus, a case can be both a precedent and part of the common law. Some precedents, however, interpret enacted law and not common-law principles. While these cases are not part of the common law, they are still precedents because they illustrate the application of a statute to a set of facts.

Generally, a judicial opinion resolves only the facts and issues raised in the action. That same opinion, however, becomes an authoritative source of law for future cases. Courts, when deciding issues, will look to those opinions for guidance. Each new decision, then, follows logically from the existing body of precedents. Each new decision becomes part of the larger body of case law and takes on precedential weight.

2. The Power of Precedent and *Stare Decisis*

The famous Latin maxim, *stare decisis et quieta non movere,* translates into "those things which have been so often adjudged ought to rest in peace." *Stare decisis* is the controlling doctrine governing the ability of judges to make law. *Stare decisis* is a principle that requires courts to follow precedent when deciding similar cases. It gives prior judicial decisions the force of law. These decisions are binding on some courts hearing later analogous cases. Courts ordinarily adhere to this doctrine and will only depart from *stare decisis* when absolutely necessary to avoid an injustice, to protect the general welfare, or to change the law to reflect contemporary values.

Stare decisis is a key maxim in American jurisprudence because it promotes stability, predictability, and fairness in the application of law. It promotes fairness because a court will treat parties with similar claims and facts in the same way. It also allows a lawyer to predict legal outcomes by analyzing prior decisions that resolve the same legal issue on the same or similar facts. If a lawyer can find controlling authority, or precedent, that speaks to her client's case, then she can anticipate how a court will likely rule in the matter. *Stare decisis* ensures stability in the law because courts are required to follow prior decisions instead of rendering decisions in a vacuum.

The power of *stare decisis* is directly related to the notion of judicial error. Generally, a party who was aggrieved by a court's mistake on a matter of law, fact, or procedure has a right to appeal that legal, factual, or procedural ruling to a higher court. If the higher court agrees with the complaining party, then the higher court may correct the error and reverse the original court's determination. A court that violates *stare decisis* by failing to apply a controlling precedent may be reversed on appeal. Hence, a court typically will honor *stare decisis* or risk a higher court reversing its holding or ruling on appeal.

Stare decisis and precedent are related, but different, concepts. *Stare decisis* requires courts to follow prior decisions when determining the outcome of like cases. Precedent is the prior decision itself.

For example, in *Palsgraf v. Long Island Railroad,* 162 N.E. 99 (N.Y. 1928), a railway company's conductor pushed a passenger carrying a package of fireworks. The conductor did not know the package contained fireworks. The package fell. As a result, the fireworks exploded, causing a shockwave, which knocked down heavy scales located at the other end of the train platform. The scales struck the plaintiff, causing injury. The plaintiff sued to recover for her damages. The New York Court of Appeals, the court of last resort in New York, held that there is no duty, hence no liability, to an unforeseen victim of negligence. The court held that the defendant could not have foreseen injuring the plaintiff, and was, therefore, not liable.

By itself, the *Palsgraf* opinion decided the outcome of one case. The holding is legally binding only on the parties in the lawsuit. The court's reasoning, however, and the legal rules employed to determine the outcome of that case, are binding on everyone within that court's jurisdiction. Under the doctrine of *stare decisis, Palsgraf* became a precedent. After *Palsgraf,* New York courts were required to look to that case to decide any lawsuit that raised the same legal issue with the same or similar facts. Why? *Stare decisis et quieta non movere*—once properly decided, a legal issue should not be decided again. If a later trial court chooses to ignore *Palsgraf* and hold that a defendant is liable to an unforeseen plaintiff, then a higher court could reverse the trial court to correct the mistake. As such, the *Palsgraf* opinion became a predictable and reliable basis to assess liability in future like cases.

Imagine a system without *stare decisis* or precedent. If judges decided each case without regard to prior cases, litigants would indeed be at the mercy of the court. Judges would have the power to reach conclusions without the aid of a sustainable, predictable body of law. Litigants would have no reliable basis to determine whether a particular act had any culpable consequence. Without *stare decisis* and precedent, the ability of lawyers to predict a legal result would be nearly impossible. And without *stare decisis* and precedent, a lawyer's ability to argue cases before a tribunal would be difficult, if not impossible. The stabilizing impact of precedent and *stare decisis* is integral to the foundations of legal analysis.

C. Hierarchy of Courts

The authoritative weight, or value, of a particular precedent depends on which court within the *hierarchy* of courts rendered the opinion. A hierarchy represents the different levels of courts within a jurisdiction. The federal court system and the court systems of most states consist of three levels: a trial court, an intermediate court of appeals, and a court of last resort. A court is bound by a decision of a higher court within its line of appeal. A decision rendered by a court of last resort, the highest court of appeals within a jurisdiction, is binding on all other courts within that same jurisdiction. A decision by an intermediate appellate court is binding on a trial court when the highest court of appeals is silent or has not conclusively decided an issue.

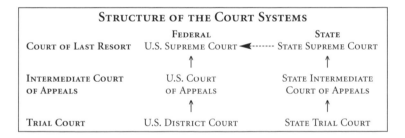

STRUCTURE OF THE COURT SYSTEMS		
	FEDERAL	STATE
COURT OF LAST RESORT	U.S. SUPREME COURT ◄-------	STATE SUPREME COURT
	↑	↑
INTERMEDIATE COURT OF APPEALS	U.S. COURT OF APPEALS	STATE INTERMEDIATE COURT OF APPEALS
	↑	↑
TRIAL COURT	U.S. DISTRICT COURT	STATE TRIAL COURT

Under our system of federalism, each state and the federal system is an independent, autonomous, and sovereign judicial system with one important exception—the United States Supreme Court. An opinion of the United States Supreme Court interpreting federal law is binding on every court in the United States, both federal and state, because it is the highest court in the land deciding a question of federal law. A decision rendered by a state's highest court of appeals, however, is usually the last word on most state issues.

Consider the following scenarios:

An Arizona trial court is bound by decisions of Arizona's highest court of appeals; Arizona's intermediate court of appeals, when the state's highest court of appeals is silent on an issue; and the United States Supreme Court interpreting federal law.

The Connecticut trial court is bound by Connecticut's highest court of appeals; the Connecticut intermediate court of appeals, when the state's highest court of appeals is silent; and the United States Supreme Court interpreting federal law.

A federal trial court considering a federal issue is bound by the United States Circuit Court of Appeals for the circuit in which the federal trial court is located and the United States Supreme Court.

D. Jurisdiction

Stare decisis requires courts to look to previous decisions, or precedent, for authoritative guidance in resolving legal disputes. Not all courts, however, are bound by every authoritative precedent. Jurisdiction is an important limit on the precedential impact of a particular decision.

Jurisdiction limits the ability of a court to exercise its authority. Jurisdiction restricts the power of a court to resolve legal issues in two ways. First, jurisdiction limits courts geographically. Second, jurisdiction limits courts by the subject matter they are allowed to consider. Geographic jurisdiction limits the power of a court to a particular territory. These limitations are drawn, for example, along municipal boundaries, county lines, or state borders. Subject matter jurisdiction limits the types of actions a court is authorized to hear. For example, a federal bankruptcy trial court does not have jurisdiction, and, therefore, cannot consider a state criminal action.

Jurisdiction limits the reach of precedent because it controls which judicial decisions, or precedents, a particular court is obliged to follow. Generally, state courts are bound only by controlling opinions derived from courts that are located within the same jurisdiction, as well as opinions derived from the United States Supreme Court when it renders a decision on federal law. For example, a trial court in Massachusetts is not bound by the opinions of the Supreme Court of Tennessee. A trial court in Massachusetts is bound by the Supreme Judicial Court of Massachusetts because that trial court is within the geographical jurisdiction of Massachusetts' court of last resort. The courts in both Massachusetts and Tennessee, however, are bound by opinions of the United States Supreme Court when it opines on federal law.

Courts may, but are not required to, follow precedent of other jurisdictions. Suppose the court of last resort in Alaska rendered a decision holding bar owners liable for injuries caused by their inebriated patrons. Subsequently, a case with similar facts alleging the same legal issue is heard by a trial court in Tennessee. The court of last resort in Tennessee has not decided the issue. The Tennessee trial court considering the issue must decide the matter and render a decision that will have precedential value for that jurisdiction. Under *stare decisis*, that decision would be binding in Tennessee until the Tennessee Supreme Court changes, reverses, or overrules the decision. The court in Tennessee could look to the Alaska court's decision for guidance, but Tennessee's court is not bound to follow that court's holding. The court, however, may be persuaded by the logic and reasoning of the Alaska court's decision and adopt all or part of that court's opinion. Alaska's decision, while not binding on Tennessee, may be persuasive.

Consider these other examples. Is the trial court of West Virginia considering a state issue bound by the court of last resort in Texas? No, because they are different jurisdictions. Is the court of last resort in New Jersey considering a state issue bound by the court of last resort in California? No, they are also in different jurisdictions. Is the court of last resort in New Hampshire considering a state issue bound by the United States Court of Appeals for the First Circuit, the federal circuit court of appeals that has jurisdiction over the federal trial court of New Hampshire? No, a state court is not bound by a federal court of appeals. Does the United States Supreme Court interpreting the United States Constitution trump all other state and federal courts? Yes, because all courts, both state and federal, are bound by the United States Constitution and the United States Supreme Court is the final arbiter of federal constitutional matters.

State courts may hear questions of both state law and federal law. A state court may consider federal law when the litigants raise a federal issue in addition to a state issue. State courts may also decide suits that raise issues of law from other states. These determinations are never binding on the other state's judiciary or the federal court because the deciding court sits in a different jurisdiction.

Federal courts may decide cases that raise federal or state issues. Federal issues arise under federal case law, federal statutes, federal regulations, treaties, or the United States Constitution. A federal district court, the trial court of the federal judiciary, has jurisdiction to hear state issues when the dispute is between citizens of different states and the amount of the claim exceeds $75,000.

In some situations, a federal court is bound by a state court's ruling. Suppose a federal court is asked to resolve a state issue. The federal court would defer to the state court's determination of the issue and not decide the issue on its own. This deference recognizes that state courts are better positioned to resolve state matters.

In other situations, a case is brought before a federal court that raises a state issue, but no precedent exists from that state's courts to guide the federal court's opinion. Perhaps the case is one of first impression or has not been conclusively decided by the state court. In these situations, the federal court either stands in the shoes of that state's court of last resort and decides the matter by interpreting state law, or *certifies* the issue to the state's highest court of appeals.

Certification, a procedure allowed only by authority of state law, allows a federal court to refer a state issue originally brought in federal court to that state's court of last resort. The state court may then conclusively decide the matter. The federal court is bound by the state court's determination of the state issue. The federal decision ultimately reached is authority for the federal court, but is not binding authority for state cases, even if a subsequent state case involves identical facts under the same law as the prior federal case. Why? The federal court and state court are independent judiciaries. Federal decisions on state law do not override decisions of a state's court of last resort. Analogous federal decisions may have persuasive impact on the state court, but are not binding.

E. Types of Authority

An *authority* refers to any cited source courts and attorneys use to oppose or support a legal proposition. Several different types of authority exist, such as cases, statutes, regulations, law review articles, legal encyclopedias, and legal newspapers. An authority can refer to either a source that is binding on a court or a source that merely persuades the court to rule in a particular way. Generally, courts and lawyers divide authorities into two groups: primary authority and secondary authority.

Primary authority is any source of law. Examples of primary authority include case law, statutes, or constitutions. Sources other than the law are secondary authority. Secondary authority is any source that comments on or editorializes about the law. Law reviews, legal treatises, newspapers, and legal encyclopedias are all examples of secondary authority.

The type of authority determines whether a source must be followed, or whether it merely serves to guide the court. Secondary authority is never binding on a court; it is only persuasive. Remember, it is not the law.

Primary authority, however, can be either binding or persuasive authority. Primary *binding* authority is any source of law that a court must follow. Primary binding authority includes any statute, regulation, constitution, or ordinance enacted in the jurisdiction, or case law rendered by the court-of-last resort in the jurisdiction. For example, a California trial court considering a state issue is bound by case law rendered by the California Supreme Court, California statutes, and the California Constitution. Primary authority from other jurisdictions is merely persuasive.

Primary *persuasive* authority is law that is not binding on a court. Primary persuasive authority can include statutes and case law from other jurisdictions. For example, a California court may look to a Nevada case for guidance, but that decision is not binding on the California court, it is only persuasive.

Persuasive authority includes primary persuasive authority, law that is not binding on a court and all secondary authority. Not all persuasive authority, however, has equal weight. Some sources are more compelling than others. Primary persuasive authority is generally more persuasive than secondary authority because primary authority is the law as opposed to a comment or opinion on the law. Even persuasive material derived from the same or similar source can have different persuasive value. For example, an article written by the seminal authority on property law would likely be more convincing to a judge than an article written by a lesser known scholar or a student. Keep in mind this simple rule—the more legally authoritative the source, the more persuasive the authority.

Consider the following sources used to support an argument before a state trial court:

An article from a legal newspaper;
An article from a prestigious law review;
An opinion from a federal court of appeals;
An opinion from the court of last resort in another state.

All of the authorities are persuasive authorities and not binding. Of the sources listed above, an opinion from the court of last resort of another state would likely rank as "most persuasive," followed closely by an opinion from a federal court of appeals. The state court's opinion was rendered by the court of last resort in that jurisdiction, not an intermediate appellate court. A federal court of appeals opinion and an opinion rendered by the highest court of another jurisdiction are more authoritative than the other sources and more persuasive because they are law. Opinions from any court usually outrank authority derived from articles or books that merely comment on the law. The law review ranks third, followed by the legal newspaper. The law review article, a scholarly commentary on the law, is more authoritative than an article merely reporting on the law.

The persuasive weight of an opinion rendered by another jurisdiction sometimes depends on how that court reached its decision. Was the persuasive opinion a unanimous decision of the court? A split decision? A court sitting *en banc*? Was a dissenting or concurring opinion included? Are you citing to that part of an opinion that bears directly on the relevant issues in dispute, or are you citing to *dicta*, the part of the opinion that was not necessary to the court's holding?

Suppose you are researching a legal issue and find three cases from another state's court of last resort that support your legal position. One decision consists of an opinion that includes a concurring opinion joined by two justices, and the proposition of law you need is found in the concurring opinion. The second decision is a unanimous opinion of the court. The third opinion consists of a majority opinion and a dissenting opinion filed by one judge, but the proposition of law you need is found in the dissenting opinion. How would you rank the persuasive weight of these authorities?

The unanimous opinion would likely rank as "most persuasive" because it represents the agreement of the entire bench on the resolution of the issue. The weight of the other two opinions is less clear. Their persuasive weight depends on the nature of the case decided and the language of the opinions filed. With that said, the concurring opinion would likely rank as "more persuasive" than the dissenting opinion because the concurrence agreed with the majority's holding albeit for different reasons. The dissenting opinion in the third case would likely rank as "least persuasive" because a dissent does not represent the law and is akin to secondary authority.

Some measure of experience is required before an attorney or student is able to accurately identify and weigh the various authorities. Sometimes the difference between authorities is quite subtle. Distinguishing between persuasive and binding sources and the relative weight of persuasive sources, however, is only one part of legal analysis. The challenge lies in crafting a meaningful way to incorporate the authority into cogent, persuasive, and well-reasoned analysis.

Practice Exercises

Complete the following exercises to reinforce your understanding of this chapter.

1. What are two sources of law in the American legal system?
2. Discuss the purposes behind *stare decisis.*
3. Consider the following questions about the court systems:
    a. What are the three levels of courts that exist in the hierarchy of the federal court system?
    b. What are the three levels of courts that exist in the hierarchy of most state court systems?
4. Answer the following questions about jurisdiction:
    a. How do courts determine what law binds them?
    b. Why must lawyers consider a court's jurisdiction?
5. Can a court amend or change language in a statute? Why or why not?
6. Explain three ways courts make law.
7. A legislator has proposed a bill that prohibits physician-assisted suicide.
    a. What stages must this bill go through before it can be passed into law?
    b. If enacted into law, can a court amend its language?
8. You are arguing a state issue before a New Mexico trial court. Which of the following cases are binding on that court?
    a. Decision from the court of last resort in Texas
    b. Decision from the court of last resort in New Mexico
    c. Decision from the federal circuit court of appeals in New Mexico
9. Identify whether the following sources are primary or secondary authority:
    a. Statute
    b. Case
    c. Legal newspaper article
    d. Legal encyclopedia article
    e. *Dicta* from a United States Supreme Court opinion

10. You are arguing a case before a North Dakota trial court. Rank the persuasive weight of the following sources:
    a. Law review article written by a law professor
    b. Legal newspaper article
    c. Decision from the court of last resort in New Jersey
    d. Dissenting opinion from the court of last resort in Indiana

Chapter 2

Rules

OBJECTIVES

WHEN YOU FINISH READING THIS CHAPTER AND COMPLETE THE
EXERCISES, YOU WILL BE ABLE TO

- IDENTIFY EXPRESSED RULES IN CASES
- IDENTIFY IMPLIED RULES IN CASES
- UNDERSTAND RULE SYNTHESIS
- DISTINGUISH BETWEEN LEGAL TESTS

A rule is a legal principle established by an authoritative body
that proscribes or governs conduct. Rules include law enacted by
legislative bodies such as statutes, treaties, ordinances, regulations,
and constitutions. Rules also include law derived from judicial
opinions, when courts render a common-law ruling or interpret
enacted law. Both enacted law and case law form the body of law
in American jurisprudence.

When a lawyer first analyzes a client's case, she typically applies
a rule or rules of law to a set of facts presented by a client. Through
this analysis, the lawyer attempts to predict how a court or tribunal would likely rule in the matter, and then, based on that objective analysis, decide how best to proceed. The rules, and how they
apply to a client's case, often determine whether a case has merit
or not. Identifying the applicable law or rule, however, can be
challenging. Rules come in a variety of guises. Some rules are enacted by a legislature, others are rendered by a court, and still others are promulgated by an administrative or regulatory agency.
Some rules, like statutes, are readily apparent. Other rules, like
some judicial rules, are not so obvious.

A. Enacted Law

Enacted laws are rules established by an authoritative act of a legislative body. Both state and federal constitutions govern how the legislative branch makes law. The enactment of a law typically requires both bicameralism and presentment. Bicameralism requires both chambers of a legislature to pass the same bill. In the federal legislative model, for example, both the House of Representatives and the Senate must each pass an identical bill. The presentment requirement commands the legislature to present the bill to the chief executive for his or her approval or veto. If both constitutional requirements are satisfied and the chief executive approves the law, then the bill becomes law.

The resulting law or statute is binding on all legal entities within the jurisdictional reach of the legislature. A state statute governs within the state's borders, and a federal statute governs the nation. If both a state statute and a federal statute cover the same subject matter, the federal statute may preempt the state statute if the subject matter is of national, as opposed to local, importance. Once enacted, the language of a statute is immutable; it can be amended only through another act of a legislature. Courts, then, are constitutionally prohibited from changing or amending statutory text—courts cannot "legislate from the bench." Courts, however, can and do interpret statutory language, particularly when the language in a statute is ambiguous or vague, and the court must construe the language in order to resolve a legal dispute.

Another form of enacted law is regulatory or administrative law. Both state and federal legislatures enact statutes that create administrative or regulatory agencies. These statutes define the goals and purposes of the agency and may authorize the agency to promulgate rules or regulations to effectuate the purposes of the statutory grant. As such, some state and federal agencies act as quasi-legislatures and promulgate regulations that carry the same force as legislatively enacted law. For example, in 1970 the federal Occupational Safety and Health Act authorized the creation of the Occupational Safety and Health Administration (OSHA) to prevent work-related injuries or death. OSHA promulgates and enforces rules on workplace health and safety that almost all employers in the United States must obey.

All enacted laws share two common and important characteristics. First, enacted law is promulgated only by an authorized legislative body. Courts and other judicial tribunals cannot enact law. Second, enacted law is immutable. Once properly enacted, a court cannot change or alter an enacted law. And while the United States Supreme Court is entitled to exercise judicial review—the power to strike down laws that violate the Constitution—the Court cannot amend statutory language by fiat. Both state and federal courts, however, may interpret or construe ambiguous or vague language in a statute or regulation to resolve a legal dispute. A court's interpretation of an ambiguous word or phrase in a statute or regulation is not enacted law, but it is law nonetheless—case law.

B. Case Law

A published case is an important source of rules. A case is a judicial proceeding between parties. A published case is a written statement by a court explaining how it reached its decision, which is published in a case reporter. While courts do not adhere to a set format when drafting opinions, a judicial opinion typically consists of seven component parts: the procedural history of the case, the factual circumstances surrounding the case, the issue(s) in contest, the holding of the court, the rules employed by the court to decide the matter, the court's reasons to support its holding, and the court's disposition of the case.

The *procedural history* of a case traces the treatment of the case as it worked its way through the court system. The *facts* consist of all the legally significant events or things that relate to the ultimate resolution of the matter before the court. The *issue* is the legal question(s) that the court is asked to resolve. The *holding* answers the question(s) presented to the court. The *rules* are the principles of law employed or adopted to resolve the issue. The *reasoning* ex-

---

Components of a Case

Procedural history: traces the case as it worked its way through the court system

Facts: describes the events, circumstances, or objects that relate to the ultimate resolution of the matter

Issue: states the legal question(s) that the court is asked to resolve

Holding: resolves the question(s) presented to the court

Rules: states the principles of law employed or adopted to resolve the issue

Reasoning: explains how the court reached its decision

Disposition: states the ultimate resolution of the matter

---

plains how the court reached its decision. Finally, the *disposition* is the ultimate settlement of the matter.

Rules in cases can be either express or implied. An expressed rule is clear and manifest in the body of the opinion. An implied rule is not articulated in the body of the opinion.

1. Express Rules

In some opinions, the court clearly expresses the relevant rules. Perhaps the issue raised in the opinion involved enacted law or a settled common-law principle. The court may also expressly articulate a rule that resolves ambiguous language in a statute or a rule that alters or informs an existing common-law principle. While not necessarily flagged as "rules" within the narrative of the opinion, expressed rules will describe a principle of law employed or adopted by the court to resolve the legal issue. Because expressed rules are clear and manifest in the body of the opinion, they generally are obvious and easy to identify. For example, consider the following opinion:

> *The issue before us today is whether the city police entrapped the defendant, John Hooks, into committing the*

crime charged. On October 6, 2007, an undercover officer from City Police Department approached the defendant on Main Street and offered to purchase a quantity of cocaine hydrochloride. According to the trial transcript, the undercover officer found the defendant waiting outside a local bar. The officer approached the defendant and said, "I'm interested in purchasing powder cocaine. Can you help me?" The defendant immediately reached into his coat pocket and produced a clear plastic bag containing a white powder. The defendant then said, "OK. Two thousand dollars." The officer handed the defendant twenty $100 bills and accepted the plastic bag in exchange for the cash. The officer then placed the defendant under arrest for the possession and sale of a controlled substance in violation of state laws 18.4.1(b) and 18.4.2(c)(1). At trial, the defendant asked the trial court judge to instruct the jury on the defense of entrapment. The trial judge refused the instruction, ruling that the evidence presented at trial failed to show that the police officer induced the defendant to commit the crime. The jury returned a guilty verdict, and the trial court judge sentenced the defendant to eighteen months in the state penitentiary.

The trial court judge correctly declined to instruct the jury on the entrapment defense. State Statute 14.3.4 allows a defendant to argue that police entrapped him into committing the crime or crimes charged in an indictment. State Code 14.3.4 (2005). The statute states, in relevant part, "if a state actor induces another to commit a crime that he was not predisposed to commit, the defendant may aver the absolute defense of criminal entrapment." Id. This court, in State v. Elliott, explained that "police must do more than merely solicit a defendant to commit a crime to allow a defendant to raise the entrapment defense." State v. Elliott, 45 State 456, 462 (1998). In this case, the undercover officer merely requested that the defendant help him to procure cocaine. This lone request is insufficient to support the entrapment defense. We affirm the decision of the trial court.

In this case, the court relied on both enacted law and case law in its opinion. First, the court described the relevant state statute on the defense of entrapment. The court then cited to an earlier precedent, the *Elliott* case, that announced a rule to determine when a state actor induces another to commit a crime. Both rules were apparent from the opinion and are thus expressed rules. The difficulty, however, lies in identifying rules of law that are not expressed clearly in an opinion.

2. Implied Rules

Unlike expressed rules, implied rules are unspoken or unexpressed principles of law employed by a court to resolve a legal issue. These rules are embedded within the body of the opinion but are not articulated. Enacted laws or laws established by an authoritative act of a legislative body rarely are unexpressed. Similarly, established common-law doctrines usually are fully expressed in an opinion. Sometimes, however, a court neglects to articulate a rule that is important to the resolution of a case. Perhaps the court did not consider the rule important enough to warrant full expression. Whatever the reason, an unexpressed rule can have the same authoritative weight as an expressed rule. Therefore, lawyers must learn to extract these rules from an opinion.

Identifying unexpressed rules in an opinion requires some measure of intellectual flexibility and creativity. Because the rule is implied and not expressed, lawyers must extrapolate the missing legal principle from the expressed parts of an opinion. For example, suppose you are invited to a friend's house for dinner. As you approach the front door to her house, you observe six pairs of shoes lined up to the side of the front door. When your friend opens the door to invite you inside, you observe that the host and the other invited guests are not wearing shoes. You quickly surmise that shoes are not allowed inside the house. The "no shoes" rule is an unexpressed rule that you were able to induce from the surrounding circumstances. The same type of intellectual analysis is required to extrapolate unexpressed rules from judicial opinions. Consider the following case:

The defendant, Jane Michaels, appeals her conviction in the state trial court for the possession of a controlled substance in violation of state law 18.4.1(b). The defendant argues that the trial court erred when it refused to instruct the jury on the defense of entrapment. On August 18, 2007, an undercover police officer posing as a drug dealer approached the defendant outside of the Quickie Food Mart on Main Street. The officer brandished his revolver, waived it in her face, and asked the defendant if she wanted to purchase marijuana. At trial, the officer testified that he was "in character" and brandished his gun to establish street credibility with the defendant. The defendant purchased a quantity of marijuana from the officer and was arrested. At trial, the defendant requested a jury instruction on the defense of entrapment, but the trial court denied that request. The jury returned a verdict of guilty, and the trial court judge sentenced the defendant to one month in the county correctional facility.

The trial court judge erred when she declined to instruct the jury on the entrapment defense. State Statute 14.3.4 allows a defendant to argue that police entrapped her into committing the crime or crimes charged in an indictment. State Code 14.3.4 (2005). The statute states, in relevant part, "if a state actor induces another to commit a crime that he was not predisposed to commit, the defendant may aver the absolute defense of criminal entrapment. The burden is on the defendant to prove that the state actor did induce the crime." _Id._ This court, in <u>State v. Elliott</u>, explained that "police must do more than merely solicit a defendant to commit a crime to allow a defendant to raise the entrapment defense." <u>State v. Elliott</u>, 45 State 456, 462 (1998). In this case, the undercover officer brandished his weapon when he asked the defendant to purchase drugs. But for the gun, the defendant may not have committed the crime. Therefore, the trial court should have allowed the jury to consider whether the officer entrapped the defendant. We reverse the decision of the trial court and remand for further proceedings consistent with this opinion.

In this case, like the previous case, the court relied on an expressed statute and an expressed case rule in its opinion. But, the court also relied on an unexpressed rule of law to reach its conclusion. The issue before the court involved the construction of the term "induces" in the state statute. According to the statute and the *Elliott* case, if a defendant satisfies his burden of proof to show that the police induced him to commit the crime, the defendant may properly raise the entrapment defense. The court in this case was asked to resolve whether the defendant met her burden. The court concluded that she had. But how? What unexpressed rule of law did the court apply to the facts of the case to determine that the police officer may have induced the crime? Like the "no shoes" rule, the trick is to think through the expressed portions of the opinion and extrapolate a rule of law that fleshes out the court's holding. Consider the following unexpressed rules derived from the opinion:

> **Rule 1:** A police officer who brandishes a gun as he requests another to commit a crime has induced the crime for the purpose of an entrapment defense.
> **Rule 2:** A state actor who uses coercion to persuade another to commit a crime has induced the crime for the purpose of an entrapment defense.
> **Rule 3:** A police officer who threatens another with death or serious bodily harm to persuade another to commit a crime has induced the crime for the purpose of an entrapment defense.

All three rules fairly express the court's implied intent to determine how a state actor unlawfully induces another to commit a crime. The first rule narrowly tracks the facts of the case. This rule, however, may be too narrowly focused on the facts. A rule is a general legal principle that a court can apply in future cases to resolve the issues presented. Because the first rule is tailored to fit the facts of one case, its applicability to future cases is questionable. The rule could be applied only to future cases where a police officer brandishes a gun as he requests another to commit a crime.

The second rule is broader than the first but perhaps too broad. It merely requires a state actor to coerce another to commit a crime. Should this rule apply, all a defendant would need to prove is some measure of police coercion, no matter how slight, to raise the entrapment defense. This rule would likely broaden entrapment beyond its intended scope. The rule also fails to consider a key portion of the case where the court opined that "[b]ut for the gun, the defendant may not have committed the crime." While the court failed to explain the significance of the gun, it is fair to extrapolate that the court believed that the threat of a gun could coerce a defendant into committing a crime.

The third rule strikes a balance between rules one and two by focusing on the significance of the gun without too narrowly focusing on the facts of the case. Under rule three, a police officer who threatens another with death or serious harm to commit a crime induces the crime. This rule fairly gauges the implied meaning of the court without broadening the scope of entrapment beyond its intended limit. The rule can also be applied to later analogous cases because it is not too factually limited in scope. Because the rule focuses on the implied significance of the brandished weapon and not the weapon itself, it could serve as a useful unexpressed rule of law.

To ensure that the rule is credible and fairly represents the meaning of the court, lawyers test the rule in other prior analogous cases. Here, lawyers apply the unexpressed rule to similar prior cases and determine whether the rule could serve as the unexpressed statement of law from the body of cases on point in a jurisdiction. In our example, a lawyer would apply rule three to all like previous cases on entrapment in her jurisdiction. If the rule works in analogous cases because it fairly represents the unexpressed meaning of the opinions, then the rule is credible and could be applied to resolve future cases.

Unexpressed rules share two important characteristics. First, they are never enacted. A court will almost always fully express enacted law in an opinion. Second, unexpressed rules are mutable. Because these rules describe the unexpressed legal significance of a court's holding, lawyers are free to extrapolate the language the court could have expressed had it chosen to fully express the rule. So long as the rule fairly expresses the court's implied meaning and so long as a lawyer cites to the originating opinion(s) to establish the authority and credibility of the rule, a lawyer can use the implied rule to the same extent as an expressed rule.

3. Rule Synthesis

As we have seen, some opinions reach a conclusion without expressly articulating a rule of law. In other instances, courts express a rule but not fully. In still other cases, a court will express a piece of a rule but other opinions are needed to complete the legal thought. Rule synthesis is a process that describes a complete expressed or unexpressed rule from its component parts. Using rule synthesis, lawyers synthesize a rule of law that incorporates the rules of several cases.

Synthesizing a rule requires extrapolating expressed or unexpressed rules from the various cases and constructing a single legal expression that covers the area. Similar to a single unexpressed rule, identifying a synthesized rule requires some measure of intellectual flexibility and creativity. The idea is to build a holistic rule from its component parts or cases. Consider the following cases:

> **Case 1**: The defendant spray-painted an obscene message on a public sidewalk. Held: The defendant is not guilty of felony mischief. Felony mischief requires a defendant to destroy private not public property.
> **Case 2**: The defendant destroyed his neighbor's mailbox after his neighbor blocked his driveway. Held: The defendant is guilty of felony mischief.
> **Case 3**: The defendant accidentally destroyed his neighbor's rose bush when the defendant installed a pool in his backyard. Held: The defendant is not guilty of felony mischief.
> **Case 4**: The defendant intentionally ran over his mother-in-law's lawn statue, after she refused to loan him money. Held: The defendant is guilty of felony mischief.
> **Case 5**: After learning that his neighbor flirted with his wife, the defendant threw a rock at his window. It missed. Held: The defendant is not guilty of felony mischief.

Case 6: The defendant had a fight with her roommate. She thought she destroyed her roommate's stereo, but it actually belonged to her. Held: The defendant is not guilty of felony mischief.

Each of these six cases deals with the crime of felony mischief. But, only Case 1 offers expressed rules. Case 1 explains that a defendant must (1) destroy (2) private but not public property. To fully express the crime of felony mischief, we must synthesize the full rule from the remaining cases. In Case 2, the defendant destroyed private property and therefore satisfies the rules expressed in Case 1. But, Case 2 also suggests that the defendant must act with ill will or malice, because the opinion included the fact that the defendant acted after the neighbor blocked his driveway. Case 3 adds credence to our "malice" rule because that court refused to convict a defendant who unintentionally destroyed his neighbor's rosebush. Case 4 appears to corroborate the "malice" rule in Case 2 because that opinion suggests that the defendant destroyed his mother-in-law's statue after she refused to loan him money. Case 5 suggests that a defendant must actually destroy property—a failed attempt is not felony mischief. Finally, Case 6 further refines the unexpressed rule in Case 5 and suggests that a defendant must actually destroy property that belongs to another. By analyzing each separate opinion, we can construct a full rule from both its expressed and unexpressed parts. Taken together, a defendant commits felony mischief when he destroys with malice the private property of another.

Then, to test the rule's credibility, a lawyer would apply the synthesized rule to each of the separate opinions she used to construct the rule as well as to any other case on point. If the synthesized rule works in analogous cases, then it fairly represents the holistic legal thought of the court. Without synthesizing the full legal expression from all the applicable authority, a lawyer would not fully understand the sometimes unexpressed parameters of a legal doctrine—a serious error.

C. Tests

A court will sometimes refer to a legal rule or principle as a "test." A test is an inquiry that determines whether a party has satisfied her burden of proof to support or defend against a cause-of-action or criminal charge. Rules are framed in several different types of tests, including the element test, the balancing test, and the totality of the circumstances test. Some tests include various parts or sub-parts, such as elements or factors. Elements are separate requirements of a test that a party must satisfy to meet her burden of proof. Factors, in contrast, are considerations that guide the court. Every factor need not weigh in favor of a party, so long as some factors do weigh in favor of a party.

1. Element Test

One type of test, the element test, is an inquiry that requires the court to consider several parts or subparts of a rule in order to satisfy the whole. Courts sometimes refer to these parts as elements. A party must satisfy each element to meet her burden of proof. For example, to commit the crime of burglary, the prosecution must prove that a defendant broke and entered a dwelling at night with the intent to commit a felony therein. This element test has four sub-parts or elements. A defendant must (1) break and enter (2) a dwelling (3) at night (4) with the intent to commit a felony therein. A court can only convict the defendant if the prosecution meets its burden on all four parts.

2. Balancing Test

A balancing test is another type of legal inquiry. A balancing test consists of several factors that a court will weigh to reach its conclusion. In a balancing test, a court will balance several considerations, looking at the quality or quantity of evidence supporting each. A very strong showing of one factor may lessen the importance of the other factor(s). Consider the following example:

Suppose a criminal defendant claimed the government violated her right to a speedy trial under the Sixth Amendment of the United States Constitution. When considering this claim, a federal trial court will balance four factors: (1) the length of the delay, (2) the reason for the delay, (3) the defendant's assertion of her right to a speedy trial, and (4) the prejudice that the defendant suffers due to the delay. The court must weigh all of these factors to determine the outcome of the case. But a stronger showing on one or more of the factors could outweigh a weaker showing on the other factors.

3. Totality of the Circumstances Test

A totality of the circumstances test is another legal inquiry that courts use to determine the outcome of cases. Unlike an element test or a balancing test that have a set number of sub-parts, a totality of the circumstances test requires the court to consider all of the relevant circumstances of a particular case and not any one circumstance. Unlike the balancing test and the element test, which provide a specific framework for the analysis, the totality of the circumstances test loosely frames the analysis by indicating the scope of the court's consideration.

Consider the following totality of the circumstances test:

A law states that criminal defendants' confessions are admissible only if they are voluntary and not coerced. To determine whether a defendant's confession is voluntary, courts apply a totality of the circumstances test. The court considers the totality of all the circumstances surrounding the confession, not merely one isolated component. For instance, the court may consider circumstances regarding the confession, such as the mental state of the defendant when he confessed, the demeanor of the officers, or whether the defendant was denied food, sleep, or counsel. Thus, the analysis is broadly framed by including all the circumstances surrounding the confession.

Practice Exercises

Complete the following exercises to reinforce your understanding
of this chapter.

1. How do attorneys identify rules in cases?
2. How does a rule frame legal analysis?
3. Answer the following questions:
    a. Name one type of legal test.
    b. Explain the test you have identified in part (a).
4. What is the difference between an element and a factor?
5. Identify the rule in the following opinion.

> *Naomi owned several acres of land. She prided herself on
> her beautiful gardens. Periodically, intruders would enter her
> property and ruin her gardens. Naomi decided to take action
> in order to protect her property. She built an electrified fence
> around her land. One night, Ariel attempted to enter
> Naomi's land. He tried to climb over the electric fence and
> suffered a severe electric shock. Ariel was hospitalized for his
> injuries and may die. He is now suing Naomi for battery.
> This court must decide whether Naomi has a defense to the
> battery claim.*
>
> *Held: Naomi is liable for battery. Naomi did not use rea-
> sonable force in this case to protect her property. Ariel's inva-
> sion of property did not threaten harm to any person, yet
> Naomi used excessive force causing serious bodily harm or
> death. Naomi's use of force to defend her property was inap-
> propriate.*

6. Identify the rule of law in the following opinion.

> *On his sixteenth birthday, John agreed to sell his bicycle to
> Ms. Lupo for one hundred dollars. Two weeks later, John de-
> cided to keep his bicycle and would not sell it to Ms. Lupo. Ms.
> Lupo sued. We hold that John did not breach the contract.
> Children eighteen years or younger cannot be held responsi-
> ble for any contract they enter into. They are too young to ap-
> preciate the magnitude of a contractual promise.*

7. Synthesize a rule for trespass from the following cases.

Case 1: The defendant entered the plaintiff's land. The defendant did not know the plaintiff owned the land. Held: The defendant is liable for trespass.

Case 2: The defendant was pushed onto the plaintiff's land. Held: The defendant is not liable for trespass.

Case 3: The plaintiff invited defendant to enter her land. Held: The defendant is not liable for trespass.

8. Synthesize a rule for the crime of conspiracy from the following cases:

    Case 1: The defendant and Todd agreed to commit a crime on the following evening. Held: The defendant entered into a conspiracy.

    Case 2: The defendant agreed to help Shelly commit a crime on the following evening, but the defendant thought Shelly was joking. Held: The defendant did not enter into a conspiracy.

    Case 3: Daniel agreed to help Paul commit a crime on the following evening. Paul was an undercover police officer who never intended to complete the crime. Held: Paul did not enter into a conspiracy.

9. Suppose a law exists that requires courts to consider several factors when determining the amount and duration of alimony. These factors include:

    • the standard of living of the parties during the marriage;
    • earning potential of the spouses;
    • contributions of spouses during marriage;
    • length of marriage;
    • income and assets of each spouse; and
    • age and health of spouses.

    You represent a client in a divorce action who is seeking alimony from her husband. A number of months before the divorce action, she discovered her husband's infidelity. She and her husband have been married for twenty years. Your client is fifty-five years old. Her husband is fifty-three years old and a college-educated accountant. Your client was a homemaker and never worked outside the home. The couple enjoyed a middle-class lifestyle. Your client has a high-school education. You seek to persuade the court to award your client alimony.

Using the law articulated above, how would a lawyer organize and frame an analysis of whether a court will award her client alimony?

10. Consider the following problem:

Your client has a fatal disease that is highly contagious and was warned about the different ways this disease can be transmitted. One way the disease could be transmitted is when bodily fluids of the infected person mix with bodily fluids of another. The more your client struggled with his illness, the more bitter he became. He felt that he was a good person and it was unfair that he should be struck with a fatal disease. He vowed that he would not die quietly and that somehow he would get revenge. One day, your client was walking down the street. A man pushed your client aside and continued walking. Your client became angry and confronted the man. They began to fight. Your client bit the man's hand. As a result, your client transmitted his fatal disease to the man. The man subsequently died.

Your client has been charged with murder. Murder is defined as the unlawful killing of a person with malice aforethought. Malice aforethought can be shown by demonstrating: (1) a specific intent to kill, (2) a specific intent to cause grievous bodily injury, or (3) in circumstances known to the defendant, a reasonable person would have known there was a substantial likelihood that death would result. Explain how you would frame the analysis of your client's case.

11. The test used to establish undue influence consists of three elements: (1) the existence of influence, (2) the exertion of influence that resulted in corrupting the mind of the deceased, and (3) the provisions at issue in a will would not have been drafted but for the influence. The plaintiff's brother inherited the bulk of their mother's estate through her will. The plaintiff claims her brother unduly influenced their mother.

How will the test for undue influence frame your analysis of this legal problem?

Chapter 3

Inductive Analysis and Analogical Reasoning

OBJECTIVES

WHEN YOU FINISH READING THIS CHAPTER AND COMPLETE THE
EXERCISES, YOU WILL BE ABLE TO

* UNDERSTAND ANALOGICAL REASONING
* IDENTIFY CRITICAL FACTS
* UNDERSTAND CASE SYNTHESIS
* UNDERSTAND THE STRUCTURE OF AN ANALOGICAL ARGUMENT
* APPLY NARROW ANALOGIES
* APPLY BROAD ANALOGIES

The unique way a lawyer analyzes legal problems has developed over many years in many courts. While seemingly combative and argumentative, legal argument requires careful analysis of a client's case and the controlling authority. Measured reason, creativity, and dispassionate logic are far more important than courtroom drama or a "smoking gun."

This chapter discusses one form of analysis—inductive analysis or analogical reasoning. Inductive analysis allows a lawyer to induce a conclusion by establishing a legal analogy between the key facts in the controlling cases and the facts in the client's case. Also called reasoning by analogy, inductive analysis focuses on the material facts of the controlling case law. Generally, reasoning by analogy includes two types of analyses: the narrow analogy and the broad analogy. Narrow analogies focus on direct fact comparisons between the controlling authority and the client's case. Broad analogies focus on the common significance of the material facts in a variety of cases and how they compare to the facts in a client's case. The nature of the action, the complexity of the issues involved, the number of controlling cases, and the facts all help to determine which analogical strategy is best suited to a particular case.

A. Analogical Reasoning

Analogical analysis focuses on fact analogies. An analogy is an inference that if two or more facts or characteristics are similar in one respect, then they will be similar in other respects. A legal analogy is an inference that if the determinative facts in the controlling authority are similar to the determinative facts in the client's case, then the holdings or legal conclusions ought to be similar.

Analogy: a logical inference that if two or more things are similar in some respects, they will be similar in other respects.

Legal Analogy: a logical inference that if two or more cases in the same jurisdiction are similar with respect to facts and legal issues, they will be similar with respect to their holdings.

Analogical analysis is grounded in the fundamental principles discussed in chapter 1. Chapter 1 explored precedent and *stare decisis*. Under *stare decisis*, once a court decides how a legal principle ought to be applied to a set of facts in a particular case, that resolution or holding ought to be repeated in subsequent like cases. Hence, a court must look to prior cases when deciding cases before it. A legal analogy contends that if the key facts found in a precedent and the key facts in your case are similar, and the legal issues addressed in both are the same, then the court should rule similarly in both cases or risk violating *stare decisis*. In cases where the facts of a controlling case and your case are not readily comparable or are dissimilar, the analogy contends that the court is not required to adhere to *stare decisis* and need not rule similarly in both cases.

While a court is free to ignore controlling authority and disregard *stare decisis*, a party aggrieved by the court's failure to apply controlling authority could appeal to a higher court to challenge the lower court's ruling. All jurisdictions have a court of appeals charged with correcting errors made by lower courts. An appellate court has jurisdiction to consider whether a lower court failed to apply the correct law in a case before it. If an appellate court decides that the lower court failed to apply the controlling precedent and the appellate court finds no good reason to change the law, then the appellate court could "correct the error" and reverse the lower court's ruling. As such, courts are inclined to follow precedent and will disregard precedent only if they have very good reasons to support the change.

1. The Three Triggers: Jurisdiction—Legal Issue—Facts

In order for a court to honor *stare decisis*, a lawyer must establish three criteria. First, a lawyer must demonstrate that the court is bound to follow a prior decision because the court sits in the same jurisdiction, or line of appeal, as the court that decided the earlier case. A party can proceed up the line of appeal so long as the higher court has jurisdiction to hear the case. As you recall, a court is only bound to follow precedent decided by a court in the line of appeal. Otherwise, the case is not controlling but is merely persuasive. A lawyer demonstrates that a case is controlling when she cites to that authority. A case citation includes information about the court that decided the earlier case. For example, if a lawyer tries a case in an Ohio state trial court, and she cites to an opinion from the Supreme Court of Ohio, *Smith v. Johnson*, 134 N.E.2d 234, 243 (Ohio 1996), she is purporting to establish the *Smith* case as controlling authority on the trial court.

Second, a lawyer must demonstrate that the legal issue decided in the earlier case is the same legal issue raised in the case-at-bar. *Stare decisis* applies only when the legal issue in both the precedent and case-at-bar are identical. If the legal issue decided in the earlier case is similar to but not the same as the issue raised in the case-at-bar, then the prior case is merely persuasive and not controlling. For example, suppose a lawsuit asks a Tennessee trial court to construe the term "part-time employee" in a state unemployment compensation statute. The lawyer cites to a Tennessee Supreme Court opinion that defined the exact term, but in the context of a state income tax statute, not in the context of the state unemployment compensation statute. That case, then, would not trigger *stare decisis* because the legal issue is not the same as the issue raised in the case-at-bar. The case is persuasive but not controlling.

Third, a lawyer must demonstrate that the facts in the case-at-bar are the same or similar to the facts in the controlling authority. Here, the determinative facts in the controlling authority must be legally analogous to the determinative facts in the case-at-bar. Facts are legally analogous if they share a common trait, characteristic, or quality. For example, if a lawyer finds a case in Tennessee that analyzes when a full-time employee qualifies for state unemployment compensation, that case could not be controlling because the determinative facts are different. The determinative fact in the case-at-bar is that the employee was part-time, not full-time. The prior case could serve as valuable persuasive authority, but a Tennessee court is not bound to follow it because the critical facts are not analogous.

2. The Analogical Model

If all three triggers are met, then a lawyer employs an analogy to argue that a prior case is or is not controlling. To establish that a case is controlling, the lawyer argues that the case was decided in the same jurisdiction, raised the same legal issue, and shares the same or similar facts as the case-at-bar. Stated above, an analogy is an inference that if two or more things are similar in one respect, they will be similar in other respects. A legal analogy is an inference that if controlling case law and the case-at-bar share the same or similar facts on the same legal issue and are located in the same jurisdiction, the court hearing the present case ought to hold similarly as the controlling case law. The hearing court ought to hold in the same way as the earlier court or risk violating *stare decisis*. Conversely, a lawyer could argue that a prior case is not controlling because one of the three triggers is absent and thus the court is not bound by *stare decisis*.

Consider the following example. In order to constitute common-law battery, a defendant must unlawfully touch a plaintiff. Suppose the senior partner of your firm asked you to determine whether a defendant committed a battery against your client when the defendant hit your client with his umbrella, causing injury. After a careful review of the applicable case law in your jurisdiction, you discover one case that is "on-point" or dispositive of your legal issue, the *Cane* case. In that case, the court ruled in favor of the plaintiff and held that when the defendant hit the plaintiff with a cane, she "touched" the plaintiff for the purposes of common-law battery. The *Cane* court reasoned that the defendant was liable even though the defendant never touched the plaintiff with her person, but with an instrumentality that was within her control.

The *Cane* case is relevant because that court considered common-law battery, the same issue raised in your case. The court held in favor of the plaintiff, a result you want. In addition, the reasoning of the *Cane* opinion is applicable to your facts. That court reasoned that a cane was an instrumentality within the control of the defendant. The cane satisfied the touching requirement of common-law battery, although the defendant never touched the plaintiff with her person. Your case also involves an instrumentality, and not a direct touching, so the *Cane* opinion is applicable to your case.

Also, the facts of your case lend themselves to a reasonable fact analogy. An analogy is appropriate in this scenario because the reasoning of the precedent is applicable to your issue, and the facts are readily comparable. A cane and an umbrella share meaningful and significant attributes. Both objects are an extension of the bearer's arm and within his direct control. If you can persuade the court that the reasoning of *Cane* is applicable to your case, and the facts in the *Cane* case are similar to the facts in your case, then under *stare decisis*, that court should rule in your favor because the two cases are legally analogous.

Bear in mind that a precedent is a double-edged sword. Both a plaintiff and a defendant can use the same case, employ an analogy, and reach dramatically different conclusions. If the precedent's holding is favorable to a client's legal position, then the lawyer aims to draw a positive analogy between the facts in the precedent and the facts in the case-at-bar. Conversely, if the holding harms a client's position, then the lawyer attempts to draw a distinction between the facts in the precedent and the facts in the case-at-bar. Both sides try to persuade the court that their position is more persuasive and better supported by the case law. The lawyer who presents the more significant comparison likely prevails. For example, the defendant could use the *Cane* case to argue that an umbrella and a cane are not similar enough to trigger *stare decisis*. The defendant could argue that because the facts are not analogous, the court is not bound to apply *stare decisis*.

Legal analogies are useful when the facts of the controlling authority, or the significance of those facts, are comparable to the case-at-bar. A lawyer makes these determinations on a case-by-case basis. Successful analogies, however, depend on two fundamental skills: (1) accurately identifying the critical facts of the controlling authority and the case-at-bar; and (2) correctly synthesizing the facts of the cases.

3. Critical Facts

Critical facts are facts from the controlling precedent that a court found important when it resolved a legal dispute. Generally, most trials involve the application of law to a set of facts, and courts apply the law only to the particular facts before it. A dispute is resolved when the court determines that a particular result is required under the law and facts of the case. A lawyer must carefully read cases to identify the facts that the court needed to reach its final determination of the matter. Those determinative facts or some characteristic of those facts can be used to draw a legal analogy between the controlling case law and a client's case.

To identify critical facts, a lawyer examines the reasoning of the controlling cases. The reasoning explains the legal basis of the court's decision. In most instances, a lawyer cannot correctly identify the key facts without first understanding how the facts relate to the ultimate disposition of the case. The reasoning of the case determines which facts are significant and important. Some facts in the precedent, although seemingly important to the deciding court, may not be critical facts if they are not germane to the court's reasoning.

Consider the following facts:

Daughter   Mother   Aunt

Suppose a prior court considered whether the words daughter and mother belonged in the same category and held that both words did fit in the same category. But what was the court's reasoning? Did the court classify the words together because of the number of syllables in each word, or perhaps because the words represent the same gender, or because of some other consideration?

Another court subsequently was asked to determine whether the word aunt belonged in the same category as mother and daughter. If the prior court based its reasoning on the number of syllables in a word, then the word aunt would not belong in the category. Based on the reasoning of the prior court, the critical fact in this scenario could be that a word is multi-syllabic. Unlike the words daughter and mother, which consist of two syllables, aunt consists of only one syllable and would not belong in the same category.

If the prior court, however, reasoned that only words that represent the same gender belong in the category, then the word aunt would belong. The word aunt would be consistent with the court's reasoning. Based on this reasoning, the critical fact in this scenario is that the words represent the female gender. Like the words daughter and mother, which represent females, the word aunt also represents females and belongs in the category.

The example above illustrates the importance of identifying the court's reasoning in order to identify the critical facts. Although the words mother, daughter, and aunt could be categorized in at least two ways, by the number of syllables or by gender, you cannot identify the critical facts without first understanding the reasoning of the court. The court's reasoning determines which facts in a case are critical or determinative.

Lawyers sometimes attempt to draw analogies to any similar fact shared by both the precedent and the case-at-bar. But *stare decisis* will apply only when a prior case is legally analogous to the case-at-bar. A case is legally analogous only when the critical facts or some characteristic of the critical facts are similar. Drawing a fact comparison using a non-critical fact by pointing to a random fact similarity is not a persuasive analogy. Consider the following arguments derived from the *Cane* case previously discussed in this chapter:

> **Argument 1:** Like the defendant in *Cane*, who carried liability insurance, the defendant in the present case also carried liability insurance.
> **Argument 2:** Like the defendant in *Cane*, who touched the plaintiff with her cane, the defendant in the present case touched the plaintiff with his umbrella.

The first argument is unpersuasive because it compares a non-critical fact. Whether the defendant in *Cane* carried liability insurance had no bearing on the ultimate disposition of the case regarding whether the defendant committed a battery. The second argument is persuasive because it does compare the critical facts of the controlling authority to the critical facts in the case-at-bar. Some lawyers may be tempted to compare the holding or conclusion of a case instead of comparing the critical facts. This analysis is illogical. A legal analogy compares the facts of a decided case to the facts of your case. *stare decisis* is triggered when the facts are legally analogous. Hence, an argument should not compare conclusions or holdings; instead, it should compare facts that compel a holding.

Consider the following arguments derived from the *Cane* case:

> **Argument 1:** The Court will likely hold that the defendant is liable because like the defendant in *Cane*, who was liable when she touched the plaintiff with her cane, the defendant in the present case touched the plaintiff with his umbrella.
> **Argument 2:** The Court will likely hold in favor of the plaintiff because like the defendant in *Cane* who was li-

able to the plaintiff, the defendant in the present case is also liable to the plaintiff.

The second argument is unpersuasive. Instead of comparing critical facts, it merely requests a particular result. The lawyer is merely asking the court to find in favor of the plaintiff because some other case also found in favor of a plaintiff. The lawyer is not demonstrating any reason why the court is required, under *stare decisis*, to follow the precedent.

The first argument is persuasive. Here, the lawyer identified the critical fact and compared it to the facts of her case. The lawyer is arguing that the *Cane* holding must apply because the key facts, a cane and an umbrella, are legally analogous. Therefore, under *stare decisis*, the court should find that the defendant is liable to the plaintiff.

Unlike the *Cane* example, cases rarely turn on one critical fact derived from one case. Comprehensive analysis requires an examination of all the critical facts in a case. Courts usually weigh a variety of sometimes disparate facts when reaching a decision. Some controlling authority may include both favorable facts and unfavorable facts. In these situations, the court may conclude that one fact or a group of facts outweighs others. Careful and repeated readings of the cases help a lawyer differentiate highly determinative facts from less determinative facts in each case.

Moreover, the *Cane* example analyzed only one case. Comprehensive legal analysis, however, rarely relies on one precedent. Often a lawyer analyzes a number of cases, analogizing to some while distinguishing others. One technique that allows a lawyer to analyze several cases at once is called case synthesis. Case synthesis permits a lawyer to incorporate an entire body of law into a concise and comprehensive analysis.

4. Case Synthesis

Case synthesis is related to rule synthesis previously discussed in chapter 2. Both skills require an examination of the body of case law that addresses a particular issue. Rule synthesis blends several cases to form one holistic rule. Case synthesis blends several cases to identify a common factual denominator among the controlling authority that can serve as the basis of an analogy.

For many legal issues, a lawyer finds numerous opinions that are on-point or dispositive of a legal issue. While the number of cases may seem overwhelming, case synthesis is an effective tool that allows a lawyer to integrate a large body of case law into one holistic analysis. To perform case synthesis, a lawyer carefully reads the applicable opinions that are needed to resolve a legal issue. The lawyer needs to understand the critical facts, holdings, reasons, and any rules articulated in the authority. Next, the lawyer studies the critical facts to identify a common denominator or thread among the various opinions that incorporates the holdings and reasons of the various precedents. Finally, the lawyer builds a legal analogy around that common factual thread. When done properly, case synthesis allows an attorney to organize the analysis around a common factual denominator derived from the precedents, instead of organizing the analysis around individual cases.

Case synthesis requires lawyers to extrapolate the common significance among the critical facts of several cases. The idea is to study the facts until some commonality is identified. This commonality should be a characteristic that is shared by the critical facts in the analogous cases. The commonality must be germane to the reasons and holdings of the precedents. The common denominator must be legally significant and focus on the key factual quality that the cases deemed important.

To discover the common factual denominator, a lawyer analyzes the facts to find the first level of similarity between the critical facts in the controlling cases and the case-at-bar. Next, she lists the characteristics of the critical facts, abstracting from the specific to the general. Each abstraction should eliminate a specific trait without losing the legal significance of the original fact. Consider the following example:

As you recall, the senior partner of your firm asked you to determine whether a defendant committed a battery against your client when the defendant hit your client with his umbrella, causing injury. Your research revealed the following opinions:

Case 1: The defendant is liable for a common-law battery. In this case, the defendant hit the plaintiff with his wooden cane. When the defendant hit the plaintiff with a cane, she "touched" the plaintiff for the purposes of a common-law battery. The defendant is liable even though the defendant never touched the plaintiff with her person, but rather with an instrumentality that was within her control.

Case 2: The defendant is not liable for a common-law battery. Here, the plaintiff tripped over the defendant's briefcase that the defendant had placed next to him on the floor in a busy restaurant. The plaintiff suffered a broken arm due to the fall. The defendant is not liable because no part of the defendant's person was involved in the incident.

Case 3: The defendant is liable for a common-law battery. In this case, the defendant threw a stone at the plaintiff, causing injury. The defendant is liable because the stone was under the defendant's control when he threw it toward the plaintiff.

To synthesize these cases, identify the common factual denominator in the cases. The common denominator must relate to the holdings and reasons in the authority. In the above example, study the critical facts, the reasons supporting the holdings, and the holdings to identify the common denominator.

Critical Facts

Case 1: Cane→ Under control of the defendant→ Liability

Case 2: Briefcase→ Not under control of the defendant→ No liability

Case 3: Stone→ Under control of defendant→ Liability

Identify the common thread among these dissimilar critical facts that relate to the reasons and holdings of the opinions. Extrapolate the critical facts in the cases. Eliminate a specific characteristic or trait until you reach a general characteristic that is shared by the critical facts in all the cases without losing the legal significance of the facts.

Case 1	Case 2	Case 3
Held Object	Placed Object	Thrown Object
Held Instrument	Placed Instrument	Thrown Instrument
Within Control	Without Control	Within Control
↓	↓	↓
↓	↓	↓
↓	↓	↓

Objects or instrumentalities within the control of the defendant

In the example above, some measure of intellectual flexibility and creativity is required to discover the common factual thread between the objects. The commonality between Cases 1, 2, and 3 could be that a person commits a common-law battery if he unlawfully touches a plaintiff with an instrumentality under his control. This fact, then, can become the basis of a legal analogy.

Using case synthesis, you would employ a legal analogy that compares the common factual significance of the critical facts in the controlling cases to the critical fact in the case-at-bar. You would likely argue that like those cases where the defendants committed a battery when they touched another with instruments under their control, the defendant in the present case hit the plaintiff with his umbrella, an instrument under his control.

Both case synthesis and rule synthesis purport to blend the facts, reasons, and holdings of a variety of cases into one holistic legal thought. Rule synthesis blends relevant cases to develop a holistic rule of law that incorporates the facts, reasons, and holdings of the applicable cases. Case synthesis combines the facts of several cases to identify a common factual thread that relates to the reasons and holdings of the cases. Because the underlying mechanics of case synthesis and rule synthesis are similar, a properly identified common factual denominator often can be expressed as a synthesized rule. For example, in the hypothetical situation above, a lawyer could express the common factual denominator as a synthesized rule of law: a defendant who injures another with an instrumentality under his control commits a common-law battery.

B. Analogical Strategies

An analogy is a legal argument that infers a legal conclusion based on a comparison of facts between the controlling authorities and the case-at-bar. This section focuses on two analogical strategies: the narrow analogy and the broad analogy. A narrow analogy focuses on direct fact comparisons between a precedent and the case-at-bar, while broad analogies compare facts from the case-at-bar to a synthesized common factual denominator derived from the controlling cases.

1. Narrow Analogy

One analytical strategy, the narrow analogy, compares the facts in your case directly to the facts of a controlling case. Utilizing a narrow analogy, a lawyer seeks to persuade a court to reach a particular holding because the controlling case law has substantially similar facts to the facts present in the case-at-bar. After the similarity is identified and the reasoning of the precedent is applied to the facts of your case, the argument concludes that the court should reach the same holding as the prior case or risk violating *stare decisis*. The lawyer constructs a logical paradigm that suggests if the case-at-bar and the controlling case raise the same legal issues and share the same or substantially similar facts, then the hearing court ought to reach the same holding as the prior case.

Alternatively, a lawyer also uses narrow analogies to distinguish the facts of the case-at-bar from the precedent. Here, the lawyer argues that the key facts of the precedent are distinguishable from the case-at-bar. This argument implies that the court is not obliged to follow *stare decisis* because the facts are not analogous, thus the precedent should have no bearing on the outcome of the case. Whether drawing distinctions or similarities, narrow analogies examine the critical facts of the controlling case law and compare those facts with the facts of the case-at-bar.

When constructing an argument, the objective is to persuade a court that the controlling authority is either analogous to the case-at-bar or that the controlling authority is factually dissimilar to the case-at-bar. A properly structured argument ought to fully prove the legal analogy. That argument typically requires four component parts: (1) the point of the analysis; (2) the direct or narrow fact comparison, (3) the application of the court's reasoning, and (4) a conclusion.

The Four-Part Argument: Narrow Analogy

Step One: State the point of the analysis
Step Two: State the narrow fact comparison
Step Three: Apply the court's reasoning to your case
Step Four: Conclude

---

a. Part One—State the Point of the Analysis

The first step in formulating an argument is to state the point of the argument. The point sentence of the argument is similar to stating the topic sentence of a paragraph. The point sentence introduces the reader to the topic or point of the analysis. The sentence may also describe the general reasons that support the argument's conclusion. Consider the following examples of point sentences derived from the *Cane* example:

> **Argument 1:** The defendant did commit a common-law battery because he harmed the plaintiff with an instrumentality under his control.
> **Argument 2:** The plaintiff will prevail.

Argument 2 is not a point sentence; it merely predicts the outcome of a case. The sentence did not introduce the topic of the analysis or identify the general reasons that support the argument. The first argument, however, is a point sentence. It identified the point of the argument—the defendant committed a common-law battery—and the general premise of the analysis—because he harmed the plaintiff with an instrumentality under his control.

Most legal writing is deductive in nature. A lawyer begins a written argument by first stating the point or conclusion followed by the particulars necessary to support that conclusion. The point statement offers a reference point or context through which the reader can fully understand the rest of the analysis. An argument without a point statement weakens the persuasive impact of the argument.

b. Part Two—State the Narrow Fact Comparison

The second step in formulating an argument is to state the direct fact comparison. Here, a lawyer builds the analogy by describing how the critical facts in the case-at-bar compare to the critical facts in the controlling precedent. The fact comparison should be clear, precise, and significant. The goal is to select a fact or facts that bear on the ultimate disposition of the case. Selected facts should directly relate to the reasoning of the court. When stating the narrow fact comparison, point to specific facts rather than loose generalizations or tenuous characterizations.

Consider the following arguments derived from the *Cane* example:

> **Argument 1:** The defendant did commit a common-law battery because he harmed the plaintiff with an instrumentality under his control. Like the defendant in *Cane*, who was liable when he harmed the plaintiff, the defendant in the present case also harmed the plaintiff.
>
> **Argument 2:** The defendant did commit a common-law battery because he harmed the plaintiff with an instrumentality under his control. Like the defendant in *Cane*, who was liable when he hit the plaintiff with his cane, the defendant in the present case hit the plaintiff with his umbrella.

The first argument is unpersuasive because the fact comparison is unclear, imprecise, and not related to the reasoning of the precedent. The *Cane* case considered whether the defendant harmed another with an instrumentality within his control. Merely arguing that both defendants harmed the respective plaintiffs, without specifying how, will not convince the court to follow the prior decision. The analogy should instead focus on the instrumentality of harm, rather than the harm itself.

The second argument is persuasive. It compares instrumentalities within the control of the respective defendants. It likens a cane to an umbrella. It compares the critical fact of the case-at-bar to the critical fact in the controlling case. The lawyer is building a legal analogy by showing how the cases share key attributes.

c. Part Three—Apply the Court's Reasoning

The third step in a narrow analogy explains the reasoning of the precedent and why the fact comparison is significant. Merely pointing to a fact similarity or distinction by itself is inadequate. To sufficiently argue a point of law, a lawyer must not only persuade the court that the facts are analogous, but also why that fact comparison is important to the court. The lawyer must show how the fact comparison connects to the prior court's reasoning.

The reasoning used to support an argument can be either explicitly or implicitly stated in an opinion. In some cases, a court will expressly state the reasons that support its holding. In other cases, however, lawyers must infer the reasoning that supports a court's holding. To make sure a lawyer's inference is credible or plausible the lawyer must test it back on previous cases to see if it is consistent with the rationale of those controlling cases.

Remember that a precedent is a double-edged sword. It can be used either to draw an analogy or a distinction depending on the lawyer's legal position. The distinction or analogy unfolds when lawyers demonstrate how the fact comparison relates to the reasoning of the precedent.

Consider the following arguments derived from the *Cane* example:

> **Argument 1:** The defendant did commit a common-law battery because he harmed the plaintiff with an instrumentality under his control. Like the defendant in *Cane*, who was liable when he hit the plaintiff with his cane, the defendant in the present case hit the plaintiff with his umbrella. The court will follow the reasoning of the *Cane* court, that an instrumentality within the direct control of a defendant can form the basis of common-law battery if

that instrumentality is an extension of the bearer's arm. An umbrella, like a cane, is also an extension of the bearer's arm and within his direct control.

Argument 2: The defendant did not commit a common-law battery because he did not harm the plaintiff with an instrumentality under his control. Unlike the defendant in *Cane*, who was liable when he hit the plaintiff with an object under his control—his cane, the defendant in the present case did hit the plaintiff but with an object not under his direct control—an umbrella. The court will follow the reasoning of the *Cane* court, that an instrumentality within the direct control of a defendant can form the basis of common-law battery if that instrumentality is an extension of the bearer's arm. While a cane is within the direct control of the bearer and is an extension of the bearer's arm, an umbrella is neither. An umbrella is susceptible to the forces of rain and wind and is not a direct extension of the bearer's arm.

This example illustrates how to use the court's reasoning to support a legal analogy. It also demonstrates how the same case can be used to support either party's legal position. A cane and an umbrella have both similar and different properties and characteristics. The similarities and differences, however, must relate to the reasoning of the precedent. In Argument 1, the lawyer argues that the precedent, the *Cane* case, ought to apply to the case-at-bar because the facts are analogous. In Argument 2, however, the lawyer argues that the *Cane* case does not apply because the facts are not similar enough. The lawyer who presents the more significant fact comparison that most closely connects to the reasoning and facts of the prior case should prevail.

d. Step Four—Conclude

The fourth and final step of a narrow analogy completes the argument. The conclusion typically reminds the reader of the outcome of the issue or the general demand for relief. The logical progression of the argument culminates with a conclusion.

Review both the plaintiff's and the defendant's argument in their entirety:

> **Argument 1:** The defendant did commit a common-law battery because he harmed the plaintiff with an instrumentality under his control. Like the defendant in *Cane*, who was liable when he hit the plaintiff with his cane, the defendant in the present case hit the plaintiff with his umbrella. The court will follow the reasoning of the *Cane* court that an instrumentality within the direct control of a defendant can form the basis of common-law battery if that instrumentality is an extension of the bearer's arm. An umbrella, like a cane, is also an extension of the bearer's arm and within his direct control. The court will hold that the defendant is liable for a common-law battery.

> **Argument 2:** The defendant did not commit a common-law battery because he did not harm the plaintiff with an instrumentality under his control. Unlike the defendant in *Cane*, who was liable when he hit the plaintiff with an object under his control—his cane, the defendant in the present case did hit the plaintiff but with an object not under this direct control—an umbrella. The court will follow the reasoning of the *Cane* court that an instrumentality within the direct control of a defendant can form the basis of common-law battery if that instrumentality is an extension of the bearer's arm. While a cane is within the direct control of the bearer and is an extension of the bearer's arm, an umbrella is neither. An umbrella is susceptible to the forces of rain and wind and is not a direct extension of the bearer's arm. The court will hold that the defendant is not liable for a common-law battery.

The *Cane* case involved only one issue, one case, and the application of only one critical fact. Legal analysis, however, rarely relies on one argument derived from one precedent. Typically, lawyers make arguments from a number of cases, analogizing to some while distinguishing others. Narrow analogies focus on direct fact comparisons between a precedent and the case-at-bar. The analogy is supported by the proposition that courts are bound to follow decisions that have already decided the same legal issue under the same or similar facts. Some cases, however, are not amenable to a narrow analogy. These cases might require a broader analytical strategy.

2. Broad Analogy

Although narrow analogies are effective in many cases, a broader analogical strategy may be necessary to fully analyze a legal issue. Narrow analogies examine specific critical facts in a controlling case that are closely parallel to the facts in the case-at-bar. This analytical approach requires attorneys to draw narrow comparisons focused on material facts. In contrast, a broad analogy draws general comparisons between cases that relate to but are not necessarily parallel to the critical facts. The crux of the broad analogy is not the critical fact itself, but rather a common denominator derived from the critical facts in the controlling authorities. As previously discussed, case synthesis is the process that identifies the common denominator among various precedents. Broad analogies require some measure of intellectual flexibility in order to devise persuasive arguments that incorporate less obvious comparisons.

Broad analogies are appropriate in at least two situations. First, broad analogies are appropriate when the case-at-bar raises unique or unusual facts. These cases may not have the factual characteristics necessary for a narrow analogy because facts of the cases may not be amenable to a direct fact comparison. Second, broad analogies are appropriate when the analysis requires the integration of a large body of case law. A broad analogy allows a lawyer to compare his case to the body of authority and not just a single precedent. As such, a broader analytical approach is more comprehensive and less repetitive than a more narrow approach.

Like narrow analogies, broad analogies also require a close examination of the courts' reasoning. Merely identifying some characteristic common to a critical fact in both the controlling cases and the case-at-bar is not persuasive. The comparison must relate to the underlying reasons of the controlling cases.

The broad analogy compares the common characteristic of the facts in the controlling cases to the facts in the case-at-bar the same way the narrow analogy compares the specific critical facts in a single case to the case-at-bar. The structure of both narrow and broad analogies is similar: (1) state the point of the analysis; (2) state the broad comparison, (3) apply the court's reasoning, and (4) conclude. These steps are identical to the four-part argument used for the narrow analogy, except part two focuses on a broad, as opposed to a narrow, comparison.

The Four-Step Argument: Broad Analogy
Step One: State the point of the analysis
Step Two: State the broad comparison
Step Three: Apply the courts' reasoning to your case
Step Four: Conclude

Consider the following example:

> Your client, the plaintiff, dug a well on the defendant's property. The plaintiff claims he owns the land through adverse possession. In this jurisdiction, adverse possession is a legal doctrine that awards ownership of property to a possessor who openly, actually, exclusively, adversely, notoriously, and continuously possesses the land of another for twenty years. The only issue in your case is whether your client can establish that he actually used the property—one element of an adverse possession.

You find the following opinions:

> **Case 1:** The plaintiff has not shown adverse possession of the defendant's property because she failed to satisfy the actual use element. Adverse possessors must demonstrate actual use of the property in order to establish ownership through adverse possession. Actual use is demon-

strated by acts of dominion and control by the adverse possessor. Here, the plaintiff placed a picnic table and shade umbrella on the defendant's property. This use did not establish dominion and control because the objects could be easily removed from the property.

Case 2: The plaintiff has demonstrated ownership of the property through adverse possession. Adverse possession is established when an adverse possessor demonstrates dominion and control over the contested property. The plaintiff built a three-story brick house on an unused portion of defendant's property. This structure did show dominion and control over defendant's property.

Case 3: The plaintiff has established adverse possession. The adverse possessor must show actual use of the adversely possessed property. Actual use is best shown by evidence of dominion and control over the property. The plaintiff built an in-ground swimming pool on the locus and placed numerous beach chairs around the perimeter of the pool. While the beach chairs are not evidence of dominion and control, the in-ground pool is evidence of dominion and control.

To analyze whether the plaintiff in your case satisfies the actual use element of adverse possession, identify the critical facts in the controlling authorities. In Case 1, the critical facts include a picnic table and shade umbrella. In Case 2, the critical fact is a three-story brick house. In Case 3, the critical facts are an in-ground swimming pool and lounge chairs.

Next, identify the holdings and reasoning of the authorities. The court held that the plaintiffs in Cases 2 and 3 satisfied the actual use element of adverse possession because a house and an in-ground swimming pool demonstrated dominion and control over another's property. The plaintiff in Case 1 failed to show actual use because a picnic table and shade umbrella did not establish dominion and control of the property.

Third, identify the common factual denominator between all the critical facts of the controlling authority. That commonality must relate to the holdings and reasoning of the controlling cases. As you recall, a lawyer discerns the commonality by extrapolating the common denominator among the critical facts, paying close attention to the significance the courts gave to those facts. Under the cases described above, a brick house and an in-ground swimming pool demonstrated dominion and control of the property. On the other hand, a picnic table, a shade umbrella, and lounge chairs did not exhibit dominion and control of the property. What is the common characteristic shared among these disparate facts? An in-ground swimming pool, and, by analogy, a brick house, demonstrated dominion and control because they are not easily removable from the locus. They are not easily removable because they are permanent improvements or changes to property. A shade umbrella, lounge chairs, and a picnic table did not demonstrate dominion and control because they are easily removable from the locus. They are easily removable from the locus because they are not permanent improvements to property. The common factual denominator—the basis of a broad analogy—is the permanent character of improvements made to another's property.

Using the four-part argument described above, consider the following argument:

> *The plaintiff showed actual use because he made a fixed improvement to the property. Like the plaintiffs in the controlling case, the plaintiff in the present case demonstrated the actual use of another's real property when he dug a well on the defendant's property, which is a permanent improvement on the defendant's land. The plaintiff has shown actual use of the defendant's property because the plaintiff's well is a permanent improvement that is not easily removable from the locus. As such, the Court will rule that the plaintiff has satisfied actual use, an element of adverse possession.*

Even though a well, a swimming pool, lounge chairs, a picnic table, a brick house, and a shade umbrella are not readily comparable facts, finding a common characteristic that is consistent with the court's reasoning can be used to devise effective legal arguments. In this example, a permanent improvement to property was the common characteristic shared by all the critical facts. A well, swimming pool, and a brick house are all permanent improvements to property. This characteristic also comports with the reasoning articulated by the court. The court ruled that dominion and control demonstrates actual use, one element of adverse possession. The court reasoned that improvements that are easily removable from the property do not satisfy actual use. Permanent improvements are, by definition, not easily removable and, thus, could satisfy the actual use requirement.

Narrow analogies and broad analogies are similar analytical strategies. Both use the court's reasoning and compare facts. The difference is the specificity of the facts compared. A narrow analogy compares closely parallel facts, while a broad analogy compares more general common characteristics. Deciding which strategy to use depends on the controlling cases, the specific issues raised, and the facts in your case.

Understanding narrow and broad analogies is an important step in developing the skills necessary to become an effective advocate. These strategies are not mutually exclusive. In fact, lawyers often incorporate variations of both narrow and broad analogies in a single argument.

Practice Exercises

Complete the following exercises to reinforce your understanding of this chapter.

1. Define critical facts.
2. How do lawyers identify critical facts in a case?
3. How can both a plaintiff and a defendant use the same precedent to support their arguments?
4. When is it appropriate to use narrow analogies?
5. When is it appropriate to use broad analogies?
6. Why is it important to compare a precedent to your client's case?
7. Consider the following opinion:

    The defendant and his roommate got into an argument. The defendant then lit a cigarette and used it to burn his roommate's arm by holding him down and thrusting the cigarette into his arm eight times. Held: The defendant is guilty of assault and battery with a dangerous weapon.

    An assault and battery with a dangerous weapon is a criminal battery inflicted with an inherently dangerous weapon, or an object used as a weapon in a dangerous or potentially dangerous way. Some inherently dangerous objects, such as a gun or knife, designed to inflict serious bodily harm or death, are inherently dangerous weapons. Other objects may still be considered dangerous if they are used in a dangerous or potentially dangerous manner. Considering the manner that the lighted cigarette was handled and controlled by the defendant, and the violent circumstances of the assault, we hold that the lighted cigarette was used as a dangerous weapon. Therefore, the defendant is liable for assault and battery with a dangerous weapon.

    a. What are the critical facts of the opinion?
    b. What is the reasoning of the court?
    c. What is the holding of the court?

    Your client is charged with assault and battery with a dangerous weapon. Your client was looking for a parking space in front of a store. She saw an empty parking space, and signaled with her directional to indicate that she was intending to pull into the space. Just before your client pulled into the space, another driver cut in front of your client with her car, and drove into the parking space. Your client then got out of her car and began to argue with the other driver. A scuffle ensued. Your client poked the other driver's eyes with her car keys.

    d. Draft the defendant's argument analyzing whether the court should hold that car keys are not a dangerous weapon.

    e. Draft the prosecutor's argument analyzing whether the court should hold that car keys are a dangerous weapon.

8. Consider the following:

Your client was charged with arson. You find one precedent on point. That court articulated a four-part test for arson. That test requires: 1) the intentional or reckless disregard of an apparent risk, 2) burning, 3) of a dwelling, 4) of another. The only element at issue was whether the element of burning was satisfied. The facts of the precedent revealed that a defendant started a fire that caused the charring of two walls in a building. The court held that charring was sufficient to satisfy the burning element. The court reasoned that some damage to the structure caused by fire is required. The court noted that substantial damage or destruction of the structure is not required to commit arson.

In your client's case, the only issue is whether the burning element is satisfied. Your client threw a match into a wastepaper basket. The basket smoldered. Even though smoke blackened the walls in the building, the walls were not charred. The heat from the fire activated the fire sprinklers, which doused the fire.

    a. Draft an argument analyzing why the burning element of arson is not satisfied.

    b. Draft an argument analyzing why the burning element of arson is satisfied.

9. Consider the following:

    You are prosecuting a defendant for receiving stolen property. Your research reveals that the elements of receiving stolen property are: (1) possession and control, (2) of stolen property, (3) known to be stolen, (4) by another, (5) with intent to permanently deprive the owner of the property. Your research uncovers a precedent concluding that even though the defendant did not actually possess the stolen property, the defendant still possessed stolen property when he instructed another to place it in a location that the defendant selected.

    In your case, the defendant is charged with receiving stolen property. The defendant used a telephone to fence stolen property. Fencing is when one arranges the sale of stolen property to another. The defendant never physically possessed the property. The only issue in your case is whether the defendant possessed the property.

    a. Draft the prosecutor's argument analyzing why the possession element is satisfied.

    b. Draft the defendant's argument analyzing why the possession element is not satisfied.

10. Consider the following opinion:

    Presenting the defendant with a diamond ring, the plaintiff asked the defendant to marry him. She agreed. The defendant later broke the engagement. We hold that the plaintiff can reclaim the engagement ring. The plaintiff should recover because the defendant broke the engagement.

    a. What are the critical facts of the opinion?

    b. What is the reasoning of the court?

    c. What is the holding of the court?

    Your client, the plaintiff, was engaged to be married to the defendant. The defendant later broke the engagement with your client. The plaintiff wants to recover the diamond stud earrings that he bought the defendant a month before their intended wedding. He bought her the earrings to wear on her wedding day.

    d. Draft the plaintiff's argument.

e. Can you predict how a defense attorney will distinguish the precedent? Draft the defense attorney's argument.

11. Consider the following opinion:

    The defendant was charged with involuntary manslaughter. The defendant found a revolver in an alley and brought it to work to show his friends. He did not check to see if the revolver was loaded. In jest, he pointed the revolver at a co-worker and pulled the trigger. The gun fired and killed his co-worker. The defendant is guilty of involuntary manslaughter. We reason that the defendant is guilty because a death resulted from the defendant's wanton and reckless conduct. A reasonable person standing in the shoes of the defendant would recognize the risk to human life.

    a. What are the critical facts of the opinion?
    b. What is the reasoning of the court?
    c. What is the holding of the opinion?

    Your client, a building manager, has been charged with involuntary manslaughter. A number of weeks ago, she locked the fire exit in the building she manages, hoping to prevent a rash of burglaries in the building. That night, a fire broke out in the building. Many residents were unable to escape because of the locked fire exit. One resident died of smoke inhalation.

    d. Which strategy, narrow or broad analogy, would be most effective here?
    e. Draft your client's legal argument.

12. Case Synthesis Exercise

    You are an Assistant District Attorney. The defendant is charged with receiving stolen property. She is challenging the police's search and seizure of a handwritten note she posted on the front door of her apartment. The note advertised the sale of a car and listed the defendant's name and phone number. The defendant knew the car was stolen. The police seized the note in order to prove that the defendant possessed the stolen car, an element of the offense. The defendant claims that the police violated her Fourth Amendment right against unreasonable searches and seizures.

Your research revealed the following opinions:

Case A: The defendant cannot challenge the government's seizure of garbage that he discarded for collection. Under the Fourth Amendment, the defendant had no reasonable expectation of privacy with respect to the garbage. To challenge a search and seizure under the Fourth Amendment, a defendant must have a reasonable expectation of privacy concerning the place searched or the object seized.

Case B: Police dogs smelled the defendant's luggage in an airport and found drugs. The smell of the defendant's luggage in the public airport, however, did not violate his Fourth Amendment right. The defendant did not have a reasonable expectation of privacy concerning the smell of his luggage, because anyone in the airport could have smelled it.

In the above example, synthesize the critical facts to identify the common denominator.

Chapter 4

Deductive Analysis
& Rule-based Reasoning

OBJECTIVES

WHEN YOU FINISH READING THIS CHAPTER AND COMPLETING
THE EXERCISES YOU WILL UNDERSTAND

* DEDUCTIVE ARGUMENT
* RULE-BASED REASONING
* THE SYLLOGISM
* THE STRUCTURE OF RULE-BASED ANALYSIS

This chapter explains how to employ deductive reasoning, also called rule-based reasoning. Unlike inductive reasoning or analogical reasoning, which structures an argument around facts, deductive reasoning or rule-based reasoning, structures an argument around a rule. Inductive analysis focuses on facts and requires a lawyer to induce a conclusion by establishing a legal analogy between case law and a client's facts. In contrast, deductive analysis requires a lawyer to apply a set of facts to a stated legal premise, like a statute or common-law rule. The application of fact to a rule allows a lawyer to deduce a conclusion.

A. Deductive Reasoning—The Syllogism

Major Premise:	X is y	All Men are mortal.
Minor Premise:	and z is x	Socrates is a man.
Conclusion:	then, z is y.	Therefore, Socrates is mortal.

The ancient Greek philosopher, Socrates, is credited with developing or at least popularizing the syllogism and the deductive reasoning model. Inductive reasoning discussed in chapter 3 allows a lawyer to arrive at (or induce) a conclusion from a series of prior events. For example, a lawyer analyzes controlling authority (the prior events) to conclude how a court would likely treat a case with the same or similar facts. Deductive reasoning allows a lawyer to deduce a conclusion from a stated proposition. Premised on logic and mathematics, the classic model for deductive analysis is called the syllogism.

A syllogism is a deductive or rule-based argument containing two premises and a conclusion. From the relationship of the two premises, you are able to infer or deduce the third proposition, called the conclusion. The syllogism is a powerful analytical tool. If the two premises are "true" and the form of the argument is correct, then the conclusion has to be true. The syllogism allows a lawyer to determine the truth (or falsity) of a purported conclusion with great accuracy. The key to mastering deductive argument is to understand the syllogistic model and the relationship between its component parts.

1. The Model

The first premise in the syllogism is called the major premise. Under the classic model, the major premise is represented as "all men are mortal." The major premise is some broad statement that describes a quality, character, property, or attribute that is true to all members of a class. In the classic model, the class is "all men." The attribute or quality is that all men "are mortal." A major premise can be any statement that describes some quality, character, property, or attribute of a group that shares some attribute. For example, "all law students read judicial opinions." Here, the attribute or property that is true of the class of law students is that they read judicial opinions. Consider the following example: All persons in custody must be given a *Miranda* warning. Here, the class is persons in custody. The members of that class all share the same attribute—they must be given a *Miranda* warning.

The second premise in the syllogism is called the minor premise. Under the classic model, the minor premise is written as "Socrates is a man." The minor premise is some characteristic of a member within the major premise. It is usually expressed as a narrow statement that is purportedly included within the major premise. For example, if a major premise states that "all law students read judicial opinions" then a minor premise could state that "Mary is a law student." Or, if our major premise states that "all persons in custody must be given a *Miranda* warning" then a minor premise could state that "John is in custody." Both Mary and John are members of the class described in the major premises.

The third and final part of the model is called the conclusion. Under the classic model, that statement is written as "therefore, Socrates is mortal." The conclusion is a statement that follows logically from the application of the minor premise to the major premise. In the syllogism, the major and the minor premises will have one common term. In the classic model, that term is "men" or "man." The common term serves as the nexus between both premises—both the major and the minor premises are related by this common term. Applying the minor premise "Socrates is a man" to the major premise "All men are mortal" compels the conclusion that "Socrates is mortal." The conclusion, then, is the logical extension of the syllogism.

Consider Mary in the example above. We know that "all law students read judicial opinions." We also know that "Mary is a law student." The term common to both the major and minor premises is "law student." That nexus allows us to conclude that "Therefore, Mary reads judicial opinions." In the custody example, we know that "all persons in custody must be given a *Miranda* warning" and that "John is in custody." By applying the minor premise to the major premise, we can conclude that "Therefore, John must be given a *Miranda* warning." The nexus or common term in this example is "in custody."

The simple logic of deductive reasoning belies its strength. If the form of the syllogism is correct and the major and minor premises are true, then the conclusion deduced from the premises also has to be true. If the premises are true, then that "truth" is logically transferred to the conclusion. A well-crafted and "truthful" syllogism is almost immune from attack. If, on the other hand, the premises are not "true" or their truthfulness is open to debate or argument, then the deductive argument is weakened and vulnerable to attack. In our "persons in custody" syllogism, we concluded that John must be given a *Miranda* warning. Suppose the United States Supreme Court concluded that not all persons in custody must be given a *Miranda* warning, but only those persons about to be interrogated. Had we built our argument around the first major premise that included "all persons in custody," then someone could refute our conclusion by attacking our major premise as "untruthful" or incorrect. Nonetheless, deductive reasoning lies at the heart of most legal argument.

2. Deductive Reasoning & Legal Argument

Deductive reasoning is also called rule-based reasoning because the argument is structured around a rule—the major premise. The major premise is a statement that describes some quality, character, property, or attribute that is common to a group or class. Similarly, a rule is a statement that describes or governs conduct or action to a particular group or class of persons or entities:

- All men are mortal
- All persons who break and enter a dwelling at night with the intent to commit a felony therein are guilty of burglary
- All charitable organizations must register with the Secretary of State
- All children under sixteen years of age must enroll in school

Because a rule behaves like a major premise, it readily lends itself to deductive or rule-based reasoning. One type of rule, a statute, is more closely associated with deductive reasoning than a case rule because of one unique characteristic of enacted law—it is immutable. A court cannot change the language of a statute. As such, a statute can serve as a very "truthful" major premise. And because the strength of the syllogism depends on the strength of the premises and a statute can serve a very "truthful" major premise, statutory analysis is closely associated with deductive reasoning.

But what about case rules? A case rule looks like a major premise and acts like a major premise, but lacks an important quality common to statutes—case rules are mutable. The common law is case law rendered in the absence of enacted law. Because no statute exists to guide a court in its resolution of a lawsuit, the court must create law to resolve the issues before it. Unlike statutes, however, a court can change the common law. In fact, a common-law rule changes if only slightly every time a court considers a new set of facts against an existing precedent. Because case law is mutable, it may not serve as a very "truthful" major premise. Consider the following deductive argument based on the ruling in the *Cane* case:

> **Major Premise:** A defendant who touches a plaintiff with an instrumentality that is under his control has committed a common-law battery.
> **Minor Premise:** The defendant touched the plaintiff with his umbrella.
> **Conclusion:** Therefore, the defendant committed a common-law battery.

The syllogism demonstrates that a case rule can be argued deductively. All of the elements of the syllogism are present—a major premise, a minor premise, and a conclusion. As discussed above, a truthful minor premise applied to a truthful major premise leads to a truthful conclusion. So, assuming that the major premise is true, and that the defendant did in fact touch the plaintiff with his umbrella, you can correctly conclude that the defendant is guilty of a common-law battery. But what if the major premise is not true or not entirely true? What if other controlling precedents modify or change the rule? What if the court decides to change the rule for this case because of its unique facts?

To attack or refute the *Cane* case argument, the defendant would likely attack the major premise. Because case law is mutable, the defendant could argue that the plaintiff's deductive argument is flawed because the major premise is incorrect. Because the major premise is incorrect, the conclusion—the defendant is guilty of a common-law battery—is suspect. The defendant would likely research for a precedent that challenges the plaintiff's major premise. Or, she could devise her own rule derived from the controlling precedent and argue that the court ought to change or modify the law. Consider the following example:

> **Major Premise:** A defendant who *unintentionally* touches a plaintiff with an instrumentality that is under his control does not commit a common-law battery.
> **Minor Premise:** The defendant unintentionally touched the plaintiff with his umbrella.
> **Conclusion:** The defendant did not commit a common-law battery.

Here, the defendant challenged the plaintiff's conclusion by attacking his major premise. The defendant is able to employ a deductive argument structured around a different major premise and conclude that she did not commit a common-law battery. Because case law is mutable and can change, a deductive argument structured around a case rule is vulnerable. Because the "truthfulness" of the major premise is suspect and open to debate, the deductive argument is weakened. In the example above, the prevailing party would likely be the party who is able to persuade a court that her major premise or rule is the more attractive legal principle. The party who persuades a court that her major premise is better presents a stronger syllogism and thus a more credible and persuasive argument.

Statutory language, unlike the language in case rules, cannot be changed by a court. Only a legislature can change the language of law it enacts. As such, a statute can serve as a stronger major premise. A deductive argument built around a statute can present a very persuasive argument. Consider the following deductive argument using a state statute:

> **Major Premise:** A driver who exceeds sixty-five miles-per-hour on any public way is fined $125.
> **Minor Premise:** The defendant drove sixty-eight miles-per-hour on State Road 4.

Conclusion: The defendant is fined $125.

Assuming the major and minor premises are true, the conclusion is irrefutable. The defendant cannot advance an argument, based on the statute, that he should not be fined. Unlike a deductive argument structured around a case rule, the defendant cannot attack the major premise or offer an alternative or modified major premise to plead his case. The permanent nature of enacted law allows a lawyer to craft a deductive argument structured around a very truthful major premise.

But not all enacted law qualifies as an immutable and truthful major premise. Many statutes are enacted with ambiguous or vague language. Before a court can apply a statute to a set of facts, it must determine what the legislature meant by the ambiguous word or phrase. A court's interpretation of ambiguous statutory language is a rule—a case rule. Thus, while the statute itself is immutable, the rule that defines an ambiguous word or phrase in a statute is mutable. A court can change or modify its interpretation of ambiguous statutory language.

A major premise in a deductive argument is weakened to the extent that the statute serving as the major premise is ambiguous or vague. As we have seen, the more truthful the major premise, the stronger the deduced conclusion. A major premise without ambiguity is a stronger major premise than one full of ambiguous and vague language. A major premise with ambiguity requires a lawyer to first resolve the ambiguity in favor of her client. Ambiguity or vagueness results from unclear statutory language. Once the ambiguity is resolved, the lawyer can deduce a conclusion. Consider the following example:

> **Major Premise:** Any person who, during and in relation to any crime of violence or drug trafficking crime, *uses* or carries a firearm, shall, in addition to the punishment provided for such crime be sentenced to a term of imprisonment of not less than five years. 18 U.S.C. § 924(c) (2006) (modified from original).
>
> **Minor Premise:** The defendant bartered a gun for five kilograms of cocaine.

In this example, the conclusion cannot be determined because the major premise is ambiguous. The statute does not state whether a defendant who barters a gun for drugs "uses" the gun in violation of the statute. The word "uses" is ambiguous. It is unclear whether Congress intended a defendant to fire or to engage a gun in the commission of a crime, or whether Congress intended to include all uses of a gun, including its use in trade. The ambiguity in the statute weakens the major premise. To employ deductive reasoning, a lawyer first must solidify the major premise by resolving the ambiguity before she can deduce a conclusion. But because a rule interpreting an ambiguity in a statute is a case rule, the conclusion is vulnerable to a counter argument. Consider the following example:

The Prosecution

> **Major Premise:** Any person who, during and in relation to any crime of violence or drug trafficking crime uses or carries a firearm, shall, in addition to the punishment provided for such crime be sentenced to a term of imprisonment of not less than five years. 18 U.S.C. § 924(c)(2006) (modified from original).
>
> **Resolved Ambiguity:** Congress intended the word "uses" to mean any use of a firearm including its use in trade or barter.
>
> **Minor Premise:** The defendant bartered a gun for five kilograms of cocaine.
>
> **Conclusion:** The defendant shall be sentenced to prison under the statute.

The Defendant

> **Major Premise:** Any person who, during and in relation to any crime of violence or drug trafficking crime uses or carries a firearm, shall, in addition to the punishment provided for such crime be sentenced to a term of imprisonment of not less than five years. 18 U.S.C. § 924(c) (2006) (modified from original).

Resolved Ambiguity: Congress intended the word "uses" to mean engaging or firing a gun in the commission of the crime.
Minor Premise: The defendant bartered a gun for five kilograms of cocaine.
Conclusion: The defendant shall not be sentenced to prison under the statute.

Both the government and the defendant resolved the ambiguity by offering a definition that defines the term "uses." Each party advanced a definition that benefited his or her legal position. Both parties then employed deductive or rule-based reasoning and deduced a conclusion by applying the minor premise—the facts—to the resolved major premise—the statute. Because each argument rested on the resolution of the ambiguity in the major premise, each party is able to deduce a conclusion that favors his or her position. Ultimately, the prevailing party is the one who presents the more credible or "truthful" resolution of the ambiguous term.

3. Identifying Flaws in a Syllogism

The syllogism is premised on logic and the relationship between the major premise, minor premise, and the conclusion. If a lawyer fails to structure correctly the syllogism, the argument is flawed. A syllogism is flawed if one of the premises is incomplete or implied. In some cases, a syllogism is flawed because the major premise does not fully explain, develop, or define the law. Without a fully developed major premise, the argument fails. Consider the following example:

Major premise: A shopkeeper may detain a patron suspected of shoplifting for a reasonable period of time.
Minor premise: The defendant detained the plaintiff for ninety minutes.
Conclusion: The defendant detained the plaintiff for a reasonable period of time.

Here, the syllogism fails to address an ambiguity raised in the major premise because the major premise doesn't define the phrase "reasonable period of time." Without a fully developed major premise, this syllogism is flawed. Thus, the argument is unpersuasive and lacks credibility.

In other situations, a premise might be indirectly stated or implied. While a syllogism with an implied premise is not technically flawed, a well-developed syllogism expresses fully both premises — the major premise and the minor premise. For example:

> **Major premise:** A person who reaches sixteen years of age may apply for a driver's license to drive a vehicle in this state.
> **Conclusion:** Sean may apply for a driver's license.

Here, the syllogism lacks a minor premise — the fact that Sean has reached sixteen years of age. The reader must infer this fact from the major premise and the conclusion. Each part of a well-developed syllogism, however, should be fully expressed.

B. The Structure of a Deductive Argument Using Rule-based Reasoning

Deductive argument — also called rule-based reasoning — structures the analysis of a legal issue around a rule instead of facts. While a legal analogy is supported by a logical inference derived from the facts of cases, rule-based reasoning focuses on a legal conclusion deduced from a stated premise. The stated premise is a rule that when applied to the facts of a case resolves the issue presented. The stated premise can be an expressed rule found in a case, an unexpressed rule derived from case law, or enacted law.

A conclusion deduced from a stated premise tends to be stronger than a conclusion inferred from a fact analogy. The persuasive weight of a legal analogy depends on the significance of the facts compared and how directly those facts relate back to the court's reasoning. Ultimately, a court will judge the relative merits of the parties' legal analogies and rule accordingly. In rule-based reasoning, however, a court can agree with a conclusion deduced from a rule without having to weigh the significance of both plaintiff's and defendant's fact analogies. If the court agrees with the stated premise and how the facts apply to that premise, it will rule accordingly.

In rule-based reasoning, the objective is to describe the controlling law and then explain how the facts of a case, when applied to the law, compel a conclusion. Like a legal analogy, a properly structured rule-based argument ought to fully prove the conclusion. That argument typically requires five component parts: (1) the point of the analysis, (2) the stated premise or rule, (3) the explanation of the rule (if necessary), (4) the application of the rule to the facts, and (5) the conclusion.

The Four-Part Argument: Rule-based Reasoning
Step One: State the point of the analysis or conclusion
Step Two: State the rule
Step Three: Explain the rule (if necessary)
Step Four: Apply the law to the facts
Step Five: Conclude

---

a. Part One—State the Point of the Analysis or Conclusion

In all arguments, the first step is to state the point of the argument or the conclusion. As you recall, the point sentence introduces the reader to the topic or point of the analysis. The sentence may also describe the general reasons that support the argument's conclusion. Consider the following example derived from the adverse possession example in chapter 3. In that example, the plaintiff dug a well on the defendant's property. The plaintiff claims he owns the land through adverse possession. Adverse possession is a legal doctrine that awards ownership of property to a possessor who openly, actually, exclusively, adversely, notoriously, and continuously possesses the land of another for a term of years. The only issue in this case is whether the plaintiff can establish that he actually used the property when he made a permanent improvement to the contested land.

> **Argument: The plaintiff did actually use the defendant's property because he made a fixed improvement to the property.**

b. Part Two—State the Rule

The second step in formulating a rule-based argument is to state the rule. That rule can either be an expressed or an unexpressed rule derived from the case law, or enacted law. Suppose that after analyzing the relevant authority, you identify an unexpressed rule that defines the "actual use" element of adverse possession. That rule states that a party actually uses another's property when he makes a permanent improvement to the property.

> **Argument:** The plaintiff did actually use the defendant's property because he made a fixed improvement to the property. **To adversely possess property, a party must actually use another's property.** *Hayes v. Usmani*, 18 State 13, 17 (1998). **A party who permanently improves another's property satisfies the actual-use element of adverse possession.** *Clark v. Kent*, 30 State 24, 26 (2007); *Romantz v. Vinson*, 23 State 234, 235 (2006).

c. Part Three—Explain the Rule

In rule-based reasoning, after you state the rule, you should explain how you derived the rule unless the rule is clear, controlling, and unequivocal. If the rule is clear and unequivocal, the facts can be applied to the rule without further explanation. In many cases, however, the rule is not clear and requires explanation.

An important tenet of deductive or rule-based reasoning is the strength of the major premise—or rule. If you derived your rule from a judicial opinion or from a variety of opinions, you may need to establish how you built your rule. If the rule is derived from a piece of enacted law, like a statute or regulation, you may need to explain any ambiguous or vague provisions in the law. The purpose of explaining the rule is to establish the credibility of the rule.

In some situations, you may be able to eliminate the explanation of the rule. If the rule is a time-honored common-law principle or a piece of unambiguous enacted law, the rule may not require further explanation. For example, suppose you are analyzing a municipal property ordinance for a client who intends to build a home on a vacant lot. The ordinance states that "a dwelling shall be located at least twenty-five feet from the curb." This rule likely will not require any further explanation because it is unambiguous and clear. If, however, the ordinance stated that "a dwelling shall be located a reasonable distance from the curb," you would need to resolve the ambiguity in the ordinance and offer a rule defining a "reasonable distance." Here, you would need to explain how you derived the rule.

In our adverse possession example, the rule defining actual use was an unexpressed rule that you derived from two controlling opinions. Because you synthesized a rule from the authority, you would need to explain how you arrived at the unexpressed rule.

> **Argument[1]:** The plaintiff did actually use the defendant's property because he made a fixed improvement to the property. To adversely possess property, a party must actually use another's property. *Hayes v. Usmani,* 18 State 13, 17 (1998). A party who permanently improves another's property satisfies the actual-use element of adverse

---

1. The rule can also be explained using parentheticals:

The plaintiff did actually use the defendant's property, because he made a fixed improvement to the property. To adversely possess property, a party must actually use another's property. *Hayes v. Usmani,* 18 State 13, 17 (1998). A party who permanently improves another's property satisfies the actual-use element of adverse possession. *See Clark v. Kent,* 30 State 234, 26 (2007) (using portion of neighbor's property to store firewood does not constitute use of neighbor's property); *Romantz v. Vinson,* 23 State 234, 235 (2006) (building a pool that encroached on neighbor's property constitutes use of her neighbor's property).

possession. *Clark v. Kent*, 30 State 24, 26 (2007); *Romantz v. Vinson*, 23 State 234, 235 (2006). For example, when a neighbor built a pool that encroached on his neighbor's property, the State Supreme Court held he had actually used his neighbor's property for the purpose of an adverse possession claim. *Romantz*, 23 State at 235. In contrast, when a neighbor used a portion of her neighbor's property to store firewood, the Supreme Court held that the plaintiff did not actually use the property and held in favor of the defendant on the adverse possession claim. *Clark*, 30 State at 26. Both opinions examined the type of improvement that an adverse possessor made to a neighbor's property and focused on whether the improvement was permanent.

d. Part Four—Apply Law to Facts

Once the major premise—or rule—is described and explained, the argument continues with the minor premise—or facts. The idea is to state with specificity the facts that are required under the rule to deduce a conclusion. The facts are derived from the evidence offered at trial or from a trial record.

> **Argument:** The plaintiff did actually use the defendant's property because he made a fixed improvement to the property. To adversely possess property, a party must actually use another's property. *Hayes v. Usmani*, 18 State 13, 17 (1998). A party who permanently improves another's property satisfies the actual-use element of adverse possession. *Clark v. Kent*, 30 State 24, 26 (2007); *Romantz v. Vinson*, 23 State 234, 235 (2006). For example, when a neighbor built a pool that encroached on his neighbor's property, the court held he had actually used his neighbor's property for the purpose of an adverse possession claim. *Romantz*, 23 State at 235. In contrast, when a neighbor used a portion of her neighbor's property to store firewood, the court held that the plaintiff did not actually use the property and held in favor of the defendant

on the adverse possession claim. *Clark*, 30 State at 26. Both opinions examined the type of improvement that an adverse possessor made to a neighbor's property and focused on whether the improvement was permanent. **In the present case, the plaintiff dug a well on the defendant's property. A well is a fixed and permanent improvement to property because it is not easily removable.**

e. Part Five — Conclude

To complete a rule-based argument, the relevant facts from the case are applied to the rule to deduce a conclusion. This section demonstrates how the facts connect to the stated legal principle. The idea is to explain how the rule operates under the stated facts.

> **Argument:** The plaintiff did actually possess the defendant's property because he made a fixed improvement to the property. To adversely possess property, a party must actually use another's property. *Hayes v. Usmani*, 18 State 13, 17 (1998). A party who permanently improves another's property satisfies the actual-use test of adverse possession. *Clark v. Kent*, 30 State 24, 26 (2007); *Romantz v. Vinson*, 23 State 234, 235 (2006). For example, when a neighbor built a pool that encroached on his neighbor's property, the court held he had actually used his neighbor's property for the purpose of an adverse possession claim. *Romantz*, 23 State at 235. In contrast, when a neighbor used a portion of her neighbor's property to store firewood, the court held that the plaintiff did not actually use the property and held in favor of the defendant on the adverse possession claim. *Clark*, 30 State at 26. Both opinions examined the type of improvement that an adverse possessor made to a neighbor's property and focused on whether the improvement was permanent. In the present case, the plaintiff dug a well on the defendant's property. A well is a fixed and permanent improvement to property because it is not easily removable. **Because the plaintiff made a permanent improvement to the defen-**

dant's property, a court will likely hold that the plaintiff did actually use the property for the purposes of the adverse possession claim.

Deductive or rule-based reasoning allows a lawyer to deduce a conclusion from a stated legal premise or rule. Inductive or analogical analysis allows a lawyer to induce a conclusion by drawing an analogy between the facts of the client's case and the facts in the controlling authority. Deciding which analytical method to employ depends on a host of factors, including the facts of a client's case, the type of applicable law, the persuasiveness of the analysis, and some measure of experience and judgment. The more you practice with both analytical models, the easier it will become to decide which model to choose.

C. Deductive/Inductive Combination

Sometimes a lawyer will employ both inductive and deductive reasoning when analyzing an issue. A lawyer might want to offer an inductive argument to exemplify the deductive argument. Or, a lawyer might want to hedge her bet by analyzing the issue using both analytical strategies. To combine techniques, the relevant facts from a case are applied to the rule to deduce a conclusion and the facts from the precedent are compared to the facts of the client's case to induce a conclusion.

Consider the following example:

> *The plaintiff did actually use another's property, because he made a fixed improvement to the property. To adversely possess property, a party must actually use another's property. A party who permanently improves another's property satisfies the actual-use element of adverse possession. For example, when a neighbor built a pool that encroached on his neighbor's property, the State Supreme Court*

held he had actually used his neighbor's property for the purpose of an adverse possession claim. <u>Romantz v. Vinson</u>, 23 State 234, 235 (2006). In contrast, when a neighbor used a portion of her neighbor's property to store firewood, the court held that the plaintiff did not actually use the property and held in favor of the defendant on the adverse possession claim. <u>Clark v. Kent</u>, 30 State 24, 26 (2007). Both opinions examined the type of improvement that an adverse possessor made to a neighbor's property and focused on whether the improvement was permanent.

Deductive Argument

[In the present case, the plaintiff dug a well on the defendant's property. Because a well is a permanent improvement to property, the plaintiff actually used the defendant's land.]

[Like the pool in <u>Romantz</u>, a well is a fixed and permanent improvement to property and unlike the firewood in <u>Clark</u>, the well is not easily removable. Thus, in the present case the plaintiff did actually use another's property when he dug a well and therefore satisfies the actual use element of adverse possession.]

Inductive Argument

In this analysis, both deductive and inductive analyses are employed. Deciding when to use a single analytical strategy or when to use both depends on the complexity of the case, the issues presented, and some measure of professional judgment.

Practice Exercises

Complete the following exercises to reinforce your understanding of this chapter.

1. What are the five component parts of a typical rule-based argument?

2. Review the syllogism below and deduce a conclusion.

   Main Premise: To enroll in kindergarten at a public school in this state, a child must be five years old by September 1 of that academic year.

   Minor Premise: Emily was born on August 20 of that academic year.

   Conclusion: ?

3. Review the syllogism below and deduce a conclusion

   Main Premise: To include pictures of a student on the school's website, the school must have written permission from the child's parent.

   Minor Premise: Michael's parent has given written permission.

   Conclusion: ?

4. Review the major premise in this deductive argument and identify what is the ambiguity (if any) that needs to be resolved.

   Main Premise: Students may ride the school bus for free if they live within a reasonable distance from school.

5. Review the major premise in this deductive argument and identify what is the ambiguity (if any) that needs to be resolved.

   Main Premise: A student must purchase all necessary school supplies before the start of classes.

6. How is rule-based reasoning different from analogical reasoning?

7. Identify why the following syllogism is flawed:

Major premise: A student with a disability must receive a reasonable accommodation.
Minor premise: Charles has dyslexia.
Conclusion: Charles must receive reasonable accommodation.

8. Identify why the following syllogism is flawed:

Major premise: Students will not be allowed outside for recess in inclement weather. Inclement weather means snow, rain, or temperatures below thirty degrees.
Conclusion: On December 15, students were not allowed outside for recess.

9. When may it be unnecessary to explain the rule as one of the component parts of a rule-based argument?

Chapter 5

Statutory Analysis

This chapter discusses statutory analysis and the tools of statutory construction. Chapter 4 discussed deductive or rule-based reasoning. Under this analytical model, the argument is structured around a stated premise or rule. Employing a syllogism, a lawyer applies a client's facts to a rule or statute to deduce a conclusion. The argument's persuasiveness or credibility is premised in part on the credibility or "truthfulness" of the major premise. The more credible the major premise, the less vulnerable the argument is to attack.

A judicial rule or enacted law can serve as a major premise in a deductive argument. Judicial rules, however, are mutable or changeable. As such, a deductive argument based on a judicial rule is vulnerable to attack. An opponent could attack the major premise—the judicial rule—and devise her own argument by offering a different major premise derived from the opinions. A deductive argument, however, based on enacted law—such as a statute—is less vulnerable. Enacted law is immutable and cannot be changed. As such, a statute could serve as a credible or "truthful" major premise in a deductive argument.

Sometimes, however, enacted law has ambiguous or vague language that weakens the strength of the statute and renders the deductive argument vulnerable. An ambiguous term in a statute is a term that could have more than one meaning. For example, suppose a statute purports to regulate "banks." The term "banks" has at least two different meanings—a business that collects and loans money or the side of a lake or river. A vague term in a statute is a term that has no defined limits. For example, if a statute purports to regulate the ownership of "pets," it is unclear what animals the legislature intended to include. Most categorical terms, like "pets," suffer from statutory vagueness.

If statutory language is unclear, a court resolves the ambiguous or vague language by crafting a rule that defines the term. To argue deductively an ambiguous or vague statute, a lawyer must first advance an argument that "proves" or resolves the ambiguity in favor of her client's legal interests. Once the statutory language is no longer unclear, a lawyer applies a set of facts to the major premise—or resolved statute—to complete the deductive argument.

In order to resolve statutory ambiguity or vagueness, a lawyer must understand the various tools of statutory construction. When statutory language is ambiguous or vague, courts endeavor to interpret that language consistent with the legislature's intent when it enacted the law. A court will avoid construing a term based on its own preferences and instead will examine what the legislature intended the word or phrase to mean. Courts have developed several rules or maxims to help it glean legislative intent. With the exception of the plain meaning rule, these rules and maxims are rebuttable presumptions—courts are not required to follow any of them, but instead may pick and choose among them. The idea is that a court will choose only those rules and maxims that best determine legislative intent. Consequently, to properly analyze a statute, a lawyer must understand how a court will resolve an ambiguous or vague term in statutory language.

A. Statutory Construction

1. Plain Meaning Rule
2. Tools of Statutory Construction

1. The Plain Meaning Rule

Statutory construction begins by examining the text of a statute itself. The first step in analyzing a statute is to determine whether the language of the statute is ambiguous or vague or both. When construing a statute, courts first look to the *plain meaning* of the statutory language. Courts presume that legislators use ordinary and everyday language when they draft law. Under the plain meaning rule, courts must give unambiguous language its obvious or ordinary meaning.

The plain meaning doctrine, however, does not always control. Courts recognize two exceptions to the plain meaning doctrine. First, if a term has both an ordinary meaning and a technical meaning, a court will favor the technical meaning if the statute concerns a technical area or if the legislature intended the technical meaning. Second, if a court strictly interprets a statute according to its plain meaning, but that interpretation would lead to an illogical result or frustrate the legislature's intent when it enacted the statute, then the court may disregard the statute's plain meaning. Under this exception to the plain meaning rule, the court assumes that a legislature would not have intended the term to obstruct its purpose or lead to an absurd result. This exception to the plain meaning rule prevents a literal interpretation of a statutory ambiguity that ignores logic and fairness.

Consider the "gun for drugs" example in chapter 4. The statute increases the penalty for a person who "uses or carries a firearm" in the course of a drug trafficking crime. In the hypothetical example, a defendant bartered a gun for five kilograms of cocaine. The first step in analyzing a statute is to determine whether the word "uses" has a plain meaning. The verb "to use" means to employ, utilize, or put into action or service. Using the plain meaning doctrine, the prosecution in this case could argue that the defendant did use the gun in the commission of a crime when he bartered it for drugs. Based on the plain meaning of the language, the prosecution would ask the court to conclude that the defendant did violate the statute. But, the defendant could argue that the plain meaning doctrine ought not to apply. After reviewing the legislative record, the defendant could contend that Congress' purpose when it enacted the statute was to decrease the violence that is often associated with drug crimes. Because the plain meaning of the term "uses" includes non-violent uses of a firearm such as its use in trade, the prosecutor's construction fails to advance the legislature's intent, and thus the plain meaning of the term ought to be ignored. The defendant would argue that the term "uses" is vague because its breadth is unclear on the face of the statute. Then, the defendant would employ a tool or tools of statutory construction to prove what the legislature intended when it included the term "uses" in the statute.

2. Construing Ambiguous Statutes

When drafting a law, legislators make every effort to choose language that clearly conveys the statute's meaning and purpose. Still, statutory terms can be ambiguous or vague. Consider the following statute: *A student may not use a weapon in school.* This statute is vague. The word *weapon* is an indefinite and categorical term. It is unclear whether the legislature intended to prohibit guns, knives, scissors, paperclips, or some other instrument. To resolve the indefinite or unclear terms in a statute, a court will utilize various tools to determine the legislature's intent when it enacted the law. These tools are often based on inferences regarding how a legislature ought to behave or how language is normally used. A lawyer uses these tools to persuade a court to adopt a construction of the term that advances a client's position.

B. Tools of Statutory Construction

1. Maxims
2. Legislative History
3. Cases Construing Statutes

1. Maxims

Courts can choose among several dozen maxims (sometimes called canons) of statutory construction to help it determine what a legislature intended when it enacted an ambiguous or vague statute. A maxim is a widely accepted or generally recognized guide or custom that a court may, but is not required, to use. Each maxim is a rebuttable presumption; it can be rebutted by another maxim that the court believes better gleans the intent of a legislature. Often, a court employs a number of maxims to resolve a statutory ambiguity. Some critics contend, however, that the variety of recognized maxims allows a court to pick and choose only those maxims that corroborate the court's preference when it resolves statutory ambiguity or vagueness. Despite this, the use of maxims remains popular. The following glossary describes some of the more widely used maxims of statutory construction.

a. In Pari Materia

In pari materia is a Latin phrase meaning "on like subject matter." Statutes that are *in pari materia* share the same subject matter or legislative purpose. The maxim requires courts to construe ambiguous language in a statute consistently with other statutes on the same subject. This maxim ensures harmony within the body of legislative law by requiring coherence among similar provisions. Under this maxim, a court could examine the whole statutory code in order to maintain consistency within the code.

Suppose section 1 of a state statutory code that regulates firearms defines the term "use" as "to engage or discharge a firearm." Another section of the code, section 15, prohibits a person from "using" a firearm in the course of a felony. A court is

asked to construe the term "using" in section 15. A court construing both statutes *in pari materia* would incorporate the definition in section 1 to section 15 and limit the term "using" to
mean "engaging or discharging a firearm." The court would construe the two sections of the state's code consistently and in harmony with each other.

b. Ejusdem Generis

The maxim *ejusdem generis* is a Latin phrase meaning "of the
same kind." When a general or categorical word follows or precedes
a list of specific examples, the general term should be limited to
include only things of the same type and character as those specified in the list. This maxim limits the breadth of vague and categorical language in a statute. Suppose a statute prohibits the possession of "handguns, rifles, knives, switchblades, and other
weapons." A court is asked to consider whether a screwdriver is included within the general catchall "other weapons." Employing
ejusdem generis, the court would likely limit the construction of
the general term to mean only those things designed to cause injury or death. All of the examples that precede the catchall are designed to serve as weapons. A screwdriver is not designed to serve
as a weapon, so the court would likely exclude it from the statute.

c. Noscitur a Sociis

Noscitur a sociis is another Latin phrase that means "it is known
from its associates." Similar to *ejusdem generis*, this maxim allows
a court to construe an ambiguous term by looking at its neighboring terms for guidance. A court's application of this maxim
prevents it from giving unintended breadth to a statute's reach.
Suppose a statute prohibits a person from "brandishing, firing, or
using a firearm" in a government building. A court is asked to consider whether a person who merely possesses a firearm in a government building is "using" the firearm in violation of the statute.
Under *noscitur a sociis*, the court would look to the terms adjoin-
ing the ambiguous term and construe the ambiguous term relative
to its neighboring terms. A court would likely limit the construc-

tion of the term "using" to exclude possession since both brandishing and firing appear to require a person to engage or employ
the firearm and not merely possess it.

d. Avoid Surplusage

This maxim presumes that every word in a statute is meaningful and that a legislature would not enact law with surplus or redundant terms. When construing an ambiguous term, a court
ought to avoid a construction that would render a term redundant or immaterial. Suppose a statute prohibits a person from
"firing or engaging a firearm" in a public building. A court is
asked to consider whether an accidental discharge of a firearm is
prohibited under the statute. Using this maxim, a court could
conclude that the term "engaging" requires an intentional act. A
person must intend to engage a gun. To avoid redundancy in the
statute, the court could construe the term "firing" to include an
unintentional or accidental act. Otherwise, the term "firing"
would be surplusage.

e. Remedial Statutes

A remedial statute is a statute that cures a defect in the law or
fixes a pre-existing problem. Most civil rights legislation and labor
statutes are remedial in nature. The remedial statutes canon asks
courts to construe broadly an ambiguous statute until the statute's
remedial purpose is accomplished. Courts presume that when a
legislature enacts remedial legislation, it intends the statute to effectuate its remedial goal. As such, courts ought to interpret an
ambiguous or vague term broadly until the statute's curative purpose is served. For example, suppose a civil rights statute banned
workplace discrimination in all businesses that sell food and beverages. A court is asked to consider whether an automobile service station with a small food counter is included in the statute. Applying the remedial statutes canon, a court could broadly construe
the term "businesses that sell food and beverages" to include the
service station in order to accomplish the statute's purpose of end-
ing workplace discrimination.

f. Expressio Unius est Exclusio Alterius

This Latin phrase means "the expression of one excludes the other." When a statute includes an exclusive list of terms, this canon prevents a court from adding any additional terms. For example, suppose a statute prohibited the sale of "cocaine, marijuana, LSD, mescaline, and peyote." A court is asked to consider whether heroin is included in the statute. Applying this canon, a court would presume that by not including heroin in the list, the legislature intended to exclude it. A court, however, will not apply this canon if the list is illustrative and not exclusive. Suppose the statute above prohibited the sale of "cocaine, marijuana, LSD, mescaline, peyote and other controlled substances." The legislature added the list to illustrate the term "controlled substances." Here, a court would apply *ejusdem generis* and not *expressio unius est exclusio alterius.*

g. Presumption of Internal Consistency

A court presumes that a legislature would not enact a statute whose parts are inconsistent. So, a court will interpret a statute to promote consistency. Suppose one section of a statute prohibits a person from using a firearm in the commission of a felony. Another section of the same statute prohibits using a firearm as a weapon in a school zone. A court is asked to consider whether the term "using a firearm" in the first section includes a firearm's use in trade or barter during a drug transaction. Applying the canon of internal consistency, a court would consider the other section of the statute that limits "use of a firearm" to its use as a weapon. To ensure the statute is internally consistent, the court could rule that both sections of the statute should limit the phrase "using a firearm" to "using a firearm as a weapon." As such, the statute does not prohibit using a firearm in trade or barter.

h. Titles Are Not Controlling

Most statutes are enacted with titles that describe the general focus or purpose of the statute. Every jurisdiction, however, has laws that require statutes to include an enactment clause. The enactment clause is a statement at the beginning of a statute that certifies the statute as having the hallmark of proper legislative authority. Everything below the enactment clause is "law." When construing an ambiguous term in a statute, a court cannot rely on the language in a title because titles are not controlling. A title is not controlling because it precedes a statute's enactment clause. Suppose a statute is entitled, "An Act to Prohibit the Possession and Use of a Firearm in a Public Building." The language of the statute prohibits a person from "using a firearm" in a public building. A court is asked to consider whether a person who possesses a firearm in a public building violates the statute. Looking at the title, a court could be inclined to conclude that the ambiguous term "using" includes "possessing" because the title of the statute uses that term. But, the language in the title cannot control the construction of an ambiguous term in the body of the statute. While not controlling, the court might instead use the title as one piece of evidence of the legislature's intent when it enacted the law.

i. Constitutional Questions

This maxim, also called the Avoidance Canon, is used when two interpretations of a statute are possible, but one of those interpretations would call into question the statute's constitutionality. Under the old rule, a court was required to "save" a statute by choosing a constitutional interpretation when another interpretation would render the statute unconstitutional and thereby void. Under the modern rule, a court will avoid an interpretation of a statute that raises a constitutional question but would not necessarily render the statute unconstitutional. This maxim presumes that a legislature would never enact an unconstitutional law or even a law of questionable constitutionality. Suppose a new criminal statute increases the prison sentence for a defendant who "uses or possesses a gun" in the commission of a drug-related felony. A court is asked to consider whether the statute is a separate crime or merely a sentence enhancement for a defendant already convicted of a drug crime. Applying this maxim, a court would likely determine that the statute is a new crime because the other interpretation would likely raise serious questions under the Sixth Amendment. So, the court would avoid the constitutional questions altogether and adopt an interpretation that passes constitutional muster.

j. Lenity

The rule of lenity requires a court to resolve an ambiguity in a criminal statute in favor of the accused. Grounded in due process and fair notice requirements, the rule makes certain that a person knows the exact nature of a crime and its penalty before he or she can be convicted of that crime. If a criminal statute is ambiguous, a court should adopt a "lenient" construction that benefits the defendant. Suppose a criminal statute requires the following penalty:

(1) one year in a state penitentiary;
(2) $1000 fine;
(3) two years of probation.

A court is asked to consider whether the statute requires all three penalties or whether a sentencing court may pick among the three penalties. Applying the rule of lenity, a court would likely adopt the more lenient construction that allows a court to pick among the three penalties.

2. Legislative History

To resolve an ambiguity in statutory language, a court tries to discover what the legislature intended when it enacted a statute. Often, a court will look for evidence of intent in the statute's legislative history. Legislative history is the body of documents and transcripts created by a legislature as a bill works its way through the various stages of the enactment process. The history includes the original bill, amendments, reports, transcripts of debates, and other published records. Among the various documents, a legislative committee report is considered the most important piece of legislative history. That report is generated by a committee charged with initially reviewing and, if necessary, amending a bill. The committee report analyzes each section of a bill, discusses the purposes of the bill, and recommends whether the bill ought to be considered by the full legislative chamber. By reviewing the committee report and other sources of legislative history, a court attempts to find the reasons why the legislature enacted the law and why it used particular language to effectuate the purpose of the law.

Consider the "guns for drugs" example. Here, a statute prohibits a "person who, during and in relation to any crime of violence or drug trafficking crime, uses or carries a firearm." A defendant was indicted under the statute when he bartered a gun for drugs. A court is asked to consider whether the term "uses" includes a trade or barter. To effectuate the intent of the enacting legislature, the court decides to review the statute's legislative history. The committee report states that the original language of the bill used the phrase "brandishes, fires, or carries," and that the word "uses" replaced "brandishes, fires" because the legislators intended to penalize any use of a gun. Based on this history, the court could conclude that the term "uses" includes using a gun in barter or trade. This construction seems to better effectuate the intent of the legislators who enacted the bill.

Some judges and other commentators, however, object to a court's use of legislative history to resolve an ambiguity in statutory language. These people, called Textualists, argue that a court should look only at the language of the statute when construing an ambiguity because the enacted language in a statute is the best source of legislative intent. Moreover, these judges and commentators suspect that a statute's legislative history can be easily manipulated by legislators and courts alike. According to Textualists, a legislator could doctor the legislative history by strategically planting evidence of intent in the body of historical documents that runs counter to the majority's intent. A court could also misuse legislative history by fishing for evidence in the legislative record that corroborates the judge's own preferences but does not necessarily speak to the general intent of the legislature. A Textualist-minded jurist considering the example above would ignore the committee report and focus instead on the statute itself. Suppose another part of the statute includes the phrase "uses a firearm as a weapon." The court would likely employ *in pari materia* or *noscitur a sociis*—both textual canons—and decide that the term "uses" ought to be construed with the term "uses a firearm as a weapon." The court could then conclude that the legislature intended only to prosecute a person who uses a firearm as a weapon and a not a person who uses a firearm to barter for drugs.

Notwithstanding the Textualists' objections, legislative history is widely regarded as a reliable source of legislative intent. Often, a reviewing court will cite to a statute's legislative history and one or more maxims of statutory construction to resolve an ambiguous or vague term in a statute. In the end, a court is bound to effectuate the intent of a legislature and may use whatever tools of construction it believes will best glean that intent.

3. Cases Construing Statutes

Another way to resolve a statutory ambiguity is to research cases that interpret the ambiguous or vague language in a statute. *Stare decisis* and precedent, principles discussed in chapter 1, are also applicable to rules announced in cases construing statutes. Once a court of last resort determines the meaning of a statute, subsequent courts must follow that interpretation. Pursuant to *stare decisis*, a court's interpretation becomes precedent that other courts within its jurisdiction must follow. Although the legislature makes law by enacting statutes, courts also make law by interpreting a statute's meaning.

When construing a statute, a court first will determine whether the statutory language is ambiguous or vague. If the court determines that the language is not ambiguous, then it will apply the text's plain or ordinary meaning. If the court determines that the language is ambiguous, then it will search for evidence of legislative intent to resolve the ambiguity. That search may prompt a court to review the statute's legislative history, to apply one or more maxims of statutory construction, or examine the text of the statute. If a court of last resort construes a statutory term, then that opinion controls unless the legislature decides to amend the statutory language.

C. Statutory Interpretation and Deductive Argument

When statutory language is unclear, a court will construe the ambiguous or vague statutory language before it will apply the facts of the case to the statute to deduce a conclusion. Similarly, when advancing a statutory argument to a court, a lawyer will offer a rule that resolves ambiguous or vague statutory language in her client's favor. Once the lawyer resolves the statutory ambiguity, she applies the facts of the case to the resolved statute to deduce a conclusion.

Chapter 4 described how deductive analysis structures a legal argument around a rule. Because the argument starts with a rule, deductive analysis is also called rule-based reasoning. Most deductive arguments begin with a major premise. A major premise is a general statement that describes a quality, character, property, or attribute that is true to all members of a class. It is a general guide for conduct or action. Think "all men are mortal." The strength of a deductive argument lies with the accuracy or "truthfulness" of the major premise.

Deductive reasoning is closely associated with statutory analysis because the major premise—a statute—could serve as a very truthful major premise. Enacted law, however, can be unclear because of ambiguity or vagueness in the statutory language. To argue persuasively under a statute, a lawyer must first resolve the ambiguity. A lawyer resolves a statutory ambiguity by employing one or more of the various tools of statutory construction described in this chapter, such as the plain language rule, maxims of statutory construction, legislative history, or cases construing statutes. The point is to establish the most accurate and credible major premise to support a deductive argument.

Once the major premise is established, a minor premise is applied to the major premise. The minor premise is some element, characteristic, or member of the class represented by the major premise. It is usually expressed as a narrow statement that is purportedly included within the major premise. In the legal context, it is the facts raised in a case. Think "Socrates is a man." The conclusion is the third and final step in a deductive argument. The conclusion is a statement that follows logically from the application of the minor premise to the major premise. Think "therefore, Socrates is mortal." If both the major and minor premises are "true," then the conclusion also has to be true. Because a deductive argument is premised on logic, a deduced conclusion can be very persuasive. Consider the following deductive argument:

> **Major Premise:** No person shall possess handguns, rifles, knives, switchblades, and other weapons in a school zone.
> **Vague Term:** other weapons
> **Resolved Term:** Employing the canon *ejusdem generis*, the vague term "weapons" is limited by the preceding examples. A rifle, knife, and switchblade are designed to serve as weapons. So, the term "weapons" can only include devices designed to serve as weapons.
> **Minor Premise:** The defendant possessed a screwdriver in a school zone and used it to threaten a student.
> **Conclusion:** The defendant did not violate the statute because he did not possess a device designed to serve as a weapon in a school zone.

Statutory analysis involves many important skills. Lawyers must understand the basic syllogism and understand how to resolve ambiguous or vague terms in a statute using the tools of statutory construction. Once the term is resolved, lawyers must complete the argument by applying a set of facts to the resolved statute. Mastering these skills are important steps in understanding legal analysis—the fundamental skill.

Practice Exercises

Complete the following exercises to reinforce your understanding of this chapter.

1. How is statutory analysis different from case law analysis?
2. What is the difference between an ambiguous term in a statute and a vague term in a statute?
3. Define the plain meaning doctrine.
4. What are three sources of legislative intent?
5. Define the maxim *in pari materia*.
6. Define the maxim *ejusdem generis*.
7. Define legislative history.
8. Name one source of legislative history that is helpful in determining legislative intent.
9. A statute states: Defacing a library book is punishable by a $500 fine. Your client was caught underlining, in pencil, a word in a book she borrowed from her private school's library.
   Identify the vague or ambiguous term in the statute.
10. A statute states: A burglary is a breaking and entering of a dwelling, at nighttime, with the intent to commit a felony therein. Your client broke a window and entered a houseboat at dusk with the intent to commit a felony. He has been charged with burglary.
    Identify the vague or ambiguous term in the statute.
11. A statute regulates the sale of oranges, lemons, limes, and other fruits. Employing *ejusdem generis*, could a court conclude that apples are also regulated under the statute? Could a court conclude that apples are not regulated under the statute?
12. A statute regulates the sale of all fruits. Applying the plain meaning doctrine, how would a court hold if it was asked to consider whether a tomato is included in the statute?
13. Statute A regulates the sale of all fruits. Statute B includes tomatoes in a provision that regulates vegetables. Reading the statutes *in pari materia*, would a court include tomatoes in Statute A?

Chapter 6

Policy-based Reasoning and Other Considerations

Objectives

WHEN YOU FINISH READING THIS CHAPTER AND COMPLETE THE EXERCISES YOU WILL BE ABLE TO

* IDENTIFY POLICY
* EXPLAIN THE ROLE OF POLICY
* RECOGNIZE JUDICIAL CONSERVATISM
* TEST FOR CREDIBILITY

How a lawyer analyzes a legal problem depends on a variety of factors such as the facts of the case, the issues involved, the law, and the legal objective. You are already familiar with two modes of analysis: analogical reasoning and rule-based reasoning. Analogical reasoning identifies the determinative facts from a body of cases and then compares those facts to your client's case to induce a conclusion. Rule-based reasoning structures the analysis around a rule and then applies a client's facts to the rule to deduce a conclusion.

Beyond analogical or rule-based reasoning, legal analysis may also involve policy-based reasoning. Policy is the purpose behind the rule. Policy should be an important consideration in ensuring a thorough analysis of a legal issue. This chapter explores policy and examines policy-based reasoning. This chapter also discusses two other considerations—how to consider judicial conservatism in your analysis and how to test your arguments for credibility. A lawyer considers these concepts to ensure a comprehensive and

thorough analysis and helps prevent an overly simplistic approach
to the analysis of legal problems.

A. Policy

Policy is the purpose behind the law; it is the reason why courts
or legislators make law. Policy reflects how the law impacts society and how the law affects the well-being of the community. Because all rules purport to benefit society, policy tends to mirror the
values of society. And because a court is more prone to rule in
favor of a legal position that might promote the well-being of society and less prone to rule in favor of a legal position that might
harm society, a lawyer should demonstrate to the court how policy supports her legal position.

Consider the crime of criminal solicitation. Criminal solicitation occurs when someone requests, encourages, commands, or
hires someone to commit a crime. When the rule-maker—either
a court or legislator—criminalized solicitation, it intended to protect the public as well as punish the malfeasant. First, it sought to
protect the public from crimes committed by solicited criminals.
Second, it sought to deter criminals from inducing innocent persons to commit crimes. While the crime of solicitation prohibits
specific acts by an individual, the policy behind the law seeks to
protect society as a whole.

Policy exists in both case law and enacted law. In case law,
courts often weigh the underlying policy supporting a rule when
deciding cases. Due to the nature of precedent, each judicial decision not only affects the parties in a lawsuit, but also future potential litigants. A court recognizes that its published decisions
have a life well beyond the case-at-bar. As such, a court's decision
should further the policy behind the law involved in that case.

Legislators also carefully weigh policy considerations when enacting statutes. They enact laws to further the values and principles of their constituents. The idea for most statutes begins when
a legislator recognizes some ill to be cured or some future harm to

be avoided. The language enacted into law is simply the means to cure the ill or prevent the harm.

1. Identifying Policy

a. Case Law

Policy in case law is generally identified by looking at the reasons why the court reached its holding. If an opinion expressly articulates policy, you will generally find it in that part of the decision where the court justifies the outcome of the case. Here, the court may explain how the decision furthers the underlying purpose of the law or how the purpose protects the community. If, however, a court's opinion does not refer to the underlying policy supporting its decision, a review of prior cases that consider the issue may reveal the purposes behind the rule. Consider the following example:

> *Commonwealth v. Ramsey*: The defendant was charged with possession of illegal narcotics. He raised police entrapment as a defense. The facts reveal that an undercover police officer approached the defendant, gave him a sum of money, and asked him to purchase drugs on his behalf. The defendant declined. After persistent requests by the undercover officer, he finally agreed to purchase the drugs. The undercover officer immediately arrested him. Entrapment occurs when a government agent encourages a defendant to commit a crime that he otherwise would not have committed. Here, the defendant is not guilty because but for the repeated requests by the undercover police officer, the defendant would not have committed the crime. The entrapment defense exists to prevent police overreaching. Police officers should enforce the law and not entice an otherwise law-abiding person to commit a crime. Police officers should never plant the seed of criminality in an innocent mind.

To identify policy in the above opinion, determine the court's reasoning. The court reasoned that the defendant was not predisposed to commit the crime. Rather, he was enticed by the police. Where the court discusses its justification for its holding, it explains the policy underlying entrapment. The entrapment defense protects society by deterring police officers from abusing their power when they instigate innocent members of society to commit crimes.

b. Statutes

Sometimes, a statute may expressly state the policy or purpose underlying a law. The preamble or purposes clause in a statute may state the reasons for enacting the law. Other times, look at extrinsic sources of legislative intent. One source of legislative intent, the legislative history of a statute, can assist in determining the policy behind a statute. The legislative history of a statute consists of the documents and transcripts created as a bill advances through the different stages of the legislative process. The purpose or policy supporting the statute may have been debated at some point in the enactment process.

Other evidence of legislative intent can be found in cases that interpret a statute. When courts interpret statutes, they strive to carry out the legislature's intent when it enacted the law. To identify policy underlying a statute, identify the court's reasoning in cases interpreting that statute.

In the prior example, a lawyer could have reviewed the legislative history of the criminal entrapment statute. That review may have uncovered evidence of what the legislature intended when it enacted the crime. Or, the lawyer could have researched for legislative purpose in cases interpreting the statute. Evidence of legislative intent derived from a statute's history, however, is usually the most persuasive evidence of intent.

B. Types of Policy Arguments

1. Judicial Administration Policy Arguments
2. Normative Arguments
3. Institutional Competence Arguments
4. Economic Arguments
5. Fairness and Justice Arguments

After identifying the policy behind a rule, consider including policy arguments to support a legal argument. Or, if you are asking the court to adopt a new or modified rule, use policy to demonstrate how that rule will impact society. A legal argument analyzes the law by explaining the law and applying it to the client's case. A policy argument analyzes the underlying purpose of the law, and demonstrates how the relief sought from the court is consistent with or furthers that purpose. Policy should be researched and analyzed in all legal problems. In some cases, policy may be your strongest argument.

Legal issues can involve competing policy interests, such as privacy rights versus public safety or judicial efficiency versus fundamental fairness. When analyzing a legal issue, a court evaluates the competing policy arguments advanced by both plaintiff and defendant. Courts weigh the policy argument advanced by both parties and resolve competing policy considerations in the best interests of society at large. Therefore, it is important to anticipate your opponent's policy arguments.

The most common categories of policy arguments include: judicial administration arguments, normative arguments, institutional competence arguments, economic arguments, and fairness and justice arguments.

1. Judicial Administration Policy Arguments

Judicial administration policy arguments focus on the importance of an efficient and fair judicial system. These policy arguments tend to pit judicial efficiency against fairness to the parties. For example, courts are sometimes asked to consider the breadth of a rule or law. The party seeking a narrow and limited rule might argue that the broad rule would harm judicial efficiency by "opening the floodgates of litigation" or suggest that the broad rule might result in a "slippery slope" of endless liability. That party could argue that the proposed rule is too broad and would lead to inefficient use of court time and resources. The party could also argue that the breadth of the rule creates new liability or generates culpability that was never intended.

Courts recognize a difference between slightly extending the law and starting down a slippery slope by opening up the floodgates to litigation. A slippery slope is a court's decision that expands the law without articulating a clear limit. Courts are reluctant to change the law, especially when that change could result in endless lawsuits that clog the courts. Perhaps Justice William Grimes of the New Hampshire Supreme Court said it best when he warned that the court "let the genie out of the bottle, and it would be impossible to stuff it back in." *Corso v. Merrill*, 406 A.2d 300, 309 (N.H. 1979) (Grimes, J., dissenting). Justice Grimes focused his policy concern on judicial administration and used that policy to support a more narrow and limited rule of law.

Consider a state law that allows a family member to recover for emotional distress when he or she witnesses a defendant injure a close family member. Suppose a court is asked to consider whether a plaintiff could recover under this rule when she witnessed a defendant injure her cousin. The court may reason that if it allowed a cousin to recover, a slippery slope may result. If a cousin can recover, could a best friend recover? What about a fiancé? Where would the court draw the line? The plaintiff would likely request the court to broaden the rule to include cousins. The defendant would likely ask the court to narrow the rule to include immediate family members and exclude cousins. To resolve the dispute, the court would likely weigh the parties' competing policy considerations. The court would likely consider the need to compensate plaintiffs who suffer injury. The court would weigh this idea against its concern for judicial efficiency and the need to limit liability of the defendants who could be liable to an endless number of plaintiffs.

Judicial administration policy arguments focus on whether a rule would frustrate the efficiency of the justice system when balanced against the other considerations. If the harm to the fair and efficient administration of justice outweighs other policy concerns, a court could be persuaded to rule accordingly.

2. Normative Arguments

Normative arguments focus on social utility, such as security, public safety, or public health concerns. For example, courts in some states have allowed police to search an automobile incident to the arrest of the driver. Normally, the police must have a warrant to search a car. The normative policy supporting this exception to the warrant requirement is the court's concern that a driver may have access to weapons that could endanger the police or bystanders.

3. Institutional Competence Arguments

Institutional competence arguments focus on whether the legislature or the courts are better suited to resolve a legal issue. According to the constitution's separation of powers, the legislature creates the law and the courts apply it. Sometimes, however, a court acts as a quasi-legislature when it interprets statutes and other enacted law. Here, a lawyer might argue that a statutory question should be resolved by the legislature because the constitution gives the legislature exclusive authority to enact law. For example, suppose a state statute read "all employers must comply with the state occupational safety commission regulations." The government sued a cosmetics wholesaler when it refused to comply with the statute. The court was asked to consider whether a wholesaler who contracted with independent sales representatives was an "employer" and required to obey the statute. The wholesaler could argue that the legislature and not the court has the institutional competence to resolve the statutory question.

4. Economic Arguments

Economic arguments focus on financial considerations, such as the allocation of resources, competition, and cost-benefit analyses. Here, the court considers whether the benefits of the rule outweigh the costs of applying it. For example, suppose a court was asked to create a common-law rule that would require employers to pay every terminated employee two weeks of severance pay. Here, the lawyer for the employers would likely argue that the cost of enforcing the rule would far outweigh any benefits to terminated employees.

Economic arguments also include "deep pocket" policy that purports to spread liability among those best able to pay. For example, under the doctrine of negligent entrustment, a person is liable when he entrusts or loans a dangerous article to another person and that person injures a third party. Many cases of negligent entrustment involve a parent loaning a child a car who then uses the car to injure a third party. Under the deep pocket theory, the parent ought to be liable for the injury—even though the parent did not cause the injury—because a parent is more likely to carry insurance and thus is better able to make a plaintiff whole.

5. Fairness and Justice Arguments

A court will consider fairness, justice, and equity in its resolution of a case. Fairness and justice consider whether a judicial disposition is impartial and honest with respect to all parties. They also consider whether a disposition is free from bias or favoritism. An argument ought to consider both the merits of the case under the law and whether the client's relief is fair and just. While an argument that relies exclusively on fairness or justice without arguing the merits of the law might appeal to the court's innate sense of fair play, it will not give the court a legal basis to rule in your favor. Fairness and justice should be used to bolster a legal argument, not replace it.

After providing a solid legal foundation, an attorney may remind the court of the competing fairness interests of both parties in a case. That argument stresses that a decision adverse to a client's interest would be disproportionately unfair compared to the effect on the opponent. While a lawyer has latitude when making fairness arguments, she should focus on the impact of a court's decision on her client. For example, suppose the defendant built a garage that encroached five inches onto the property of his neighbor, the plaintiff. The plaintiff had no plans to use that part of her property. The plaintiff then discovered the defendant's encroachment. She asks the court to order the defendant to tear down his garage. The garage would have to be destroyed and built again on the defendant's land. After making his legal argument, the defendant could emphasize fairness and argue that tearing down the garage would be disproportionately unfair compared to the effect on the plaintiff. The defendant could ask the court to reach an outcome that would be fair to both parties, such as compensating the plaintiff for the encroachment but not requiring him to remove the garage. The legal argument and fairness argument combined could help the defendant win the case.

C. How to Use Policy

Four Uses of Policy
1. to support a legal argument;
2. to analyze a case of first impression;
3. to limit the scope of the law; and,
4. to expand the scope of the law.

In addition to legal arguments, a lawyer should consider making policy arguments to bolster a client's legal position. Policy-based reasoning may affect the court's decision, especially in cases involving a case of first impression or when the lawyer seeks to expand or limit the law. To engage in policy-based reasoning, a lawyer needs to identify the policy underlying a rule and show how that policy is consistent with or advances the lawyer's legal position.

1. To Support a Legal Argument

When analyzing a legal issue, consider whether your client's desired outcome would further the rule's underlying purpose. Courts generally avoid outcomes that frustrate the purpose or policy behind the law. Thus, a lawyer's argument should demonstrate that his client's position is required under the law and also furthers the policy underlying it.

For example, in some jurisdictions, the doctrine of adverse possession requires a plaintiff to possess another's property openly, exclusively, actually, adversely, notoriously, and continuously for a term of years. The policy behind this doctrine is to give a property owner sufficient notice that her ownership rights are at risk because another person is using the owner's land. Suppose the owner had five acres of wooded land behind his summer house. A possessor claims that he adversely possessed a small parcel of the owner's land for the statutory term of years, off and on. The owner could make a persuasive legal argument that the possessor did not satisfy all of the elements of adverse possession because the possessor did not continuously possess the land for the statutory term. The owner could bolster this legal argument by contending that his position fits squarely within the policy behind adverse possession. That policy is to provide sufficient notice to property owners that another is attempting to possess his property. The owner did not have sufficient notice of the adverse possession because the possessor did not continuously possess the property for the statutory term. While the legal argument looks at the legal standard and determines whether the owner can satisfy the test, the policy argument considers whether the relief that the owner requests furthers the underlying purpose of the law.

2. To Analyze a Case of First Impression

While courts are reluctant to make new law, a case of first impression may require the court to break new ground. Policy will play an important role when the court considers a case of first impression. A case of first impression is when a court has not yet considered a legal issue or when a novel set of facts is applied to an existing legal doctrine. In both cases, no controlling precedent exists to guide the court. Thus, a court will likely rely heavily on policy to resolve a case of first impression.

In cases of first impression, lawyers use policy arguments to persuade courts to adopt new law or take existing law in new directions. They advocate how a new law or the application of existing law to a novel set of facts would advance important societal goals. Consider the following example: A court is considering whether a plaintiff can sue a father who entrusted his car to his teen-aged son. The son negligently hit the plaintiff with his father's car. The jurisdiction had not yet recognized this type of extended liability called negligent entrustment. The plaintiff's lawyer could argue as a matter of law that the father wrongfully entrusted his car to his son because the father knew his son was a dangerous driver. The lawyer also could argue, as a matter of policy, that un-less the father is liable to the plaintiff, the plaintiff would not be able to collect damages because the teenaged son has no assets or insurance. Conversely, the defendant's lawyer could argue that it is unfair to hold the father liable for an injury caused by his son. Recognizing the societal benefits and detriments of this new cause-of-action, the court would decide the issue after weighing the com-peting policy arguments.

3. To Limit the Scope of the Law

Policy can also be used to limit the reach of the law. A lawyer uses policy to persuade courts to narrow the application of a law by arguing that the policy supporting the law is too broad and no longer reflects the values of society. Here, a lawyer could ask the court to narrow the law, without abolishing it.

Consider the following example: Some jurisdictions recognize common-law marriage. Common-law marriage is a doctrine that recognizes two people as married without having satisfied the statu-tory requirements of marriage. One policy supporting the doctrine is to allow surviving spouses and children to inherit the deceased spouse's estate. It also furthers traditional family values by encour-aging cohabitating couples to marry. Suppose a same-sex couple asks a court to recognize it as married under the common law. Here, the opposing lawyer could argue that common-law marriage between same sex couples would frustrate the purpose of the law to promote traditional family values. The lawyer would use policy to argue that common-law marriage ought to be narrowed to exclude same-sex couples.

4. To Expand the Scope of the Law

While policy can be used to limit the law, a lawyer also uses policy to expand it. In some cases, an existing law may fail to pro-tect society because it is too narrow. In these situations, attorneys use policy to persuade a court to expand the law to reflect current conditions.

Consider the common-law marriage example. The lawyer representing the same-sex couple could argue that the law ought to be expanded to include same-sex couples because the same-sex marriage protects the surviving spouse and children to the same extent as a common-law marriage between a man and a woman. Plus, the lawyer could suggest that society's view of traditional family values has expanded to include same-sex couples.

D. Other Considerations

In addition to policy, a lawyer should consider other influences that may affect the outcome of a case. This section discusses two factors that may impact a court's decision. First, it discusses how the conservative nature of a court could influence its holding. Second, the section discusses the importance of advancing credible arguments. A lawyer should consider these concepts to ensure a comprehensive analysis.

1. Judicial Conservatism

Courts are inherently conservative. While courts may change the law, they are reluctant to do so. One reason is because courts are bound to follow precedent, pursuant to the doctrine of *stare decisis*. The doctrine prevents courts from deciding cases in a vacuum and subtly pressures courts to conform to existing law. When a court decides a question of fact, law, or procedure, an appellate court is allowed to review that decision and determine whether the court erred. No court likes to have its decision reversed. This concern contributes to the courts' conservative nature. The more closely a court follows the precedent, the less likely its decision will get reversed on appeal. Consequently, some courts are reluctant to render rulings that push the limits of the law.

Judicial conservatism deters some courts from expressly overruling prior opinions. Instead, they express disapproval or criticism of a prior opinion or decline to endorse a prior court's holding without expressly overruling it. The court's disapproval is often subtly stated.

Understanding judicial conservatism helps lawyers craft persuasive legal arguments and anticipate legal outcomes. A lawyer should advance arguments that appeal to a court's conservative disposition. A lawyer uses the court's inherent conservatism by arguing that the client's position fits squarely within the existing law or only requires a slight modification of the law. The court will better receive this type of argument because it will not have to make new law and risk reversal on appeal.

Suppose a law regarding non-compete agreements in an employment contract allows employers to geographically restrict where their former employees can work. Employers, however, may only restrict former employees within "reasonable geographic boundaries." Courts have not explicitly stated what is considered "reasonable" or set a specific mile limit, but have consistently ruled that cases with restrictions up to twenty miles are reasonable. Your client, an employer, wants to hold its employees to a forty-mile non-compete agreement. The client has asked her lawyer to advise him whether this restriction is reasonable under the law. The lawyer determines that while the court has not defined what is "reasonable," a court might be reluctant to extend the reach of the covenant beyond twenty miles. The lawyer advises the client to stay within the twenty-mile restriction that the court has already approved. The advice is likely sound because it anticipates the court's conservative nature and does not risk asking the court to expand the law.

If a lawyer's position requires the court to change the law, she should try to persuade the court that the change is only a small extension of the existing law. An extension of the law, after all, is still a modification or change of the law. Courts are hesitant to modify established rules, but could be persuaded if the change of law is characterized as only a slight extension. Referring to the example above, suppose your client ignores his lawyer's advice and holds his employees to a twenty-five mile geographic restriction, and the employees sue your client. A lawyer could argue that this distance is reasonable. The lawyer may persuade the court that a twenty-five mile restriction is only a slight expansion of the twenty-mile geographic restriction allowed in prior cases. If a lawyer has solid reasons to support this modification of the law, the lawyer could prevail because this slight extension of existing law is compatible with the court's conservative nature. Had the client sought to double the allowable range through a forty-mile restriction, the argument would have to be quite compelling to convince a court to change the law despite its conservative nature.

2. Credibility

A lawyer should consider only credible arguments to advance his client's position. A lawyer should avoid arguments that a court may perceive as implausible. But just because an argument might not persuade a court does not mean it lacks credibility.

To test for credibility, a lawyer must ensure that an argument has a plausible basis in law and fact or a plausible basis to change or modify the law. First, a lawyer should determine whether the argument furthers or frustrates the policy underlying the law. A legal argument that violates public policy might lack credibility. Second, a lawyer must develop sound judgment to determine whether an argument lacks credibility. With experience, a lawyer develops an innate ability to test if an argument is far-fetched or fails the "smell test." The idea is to put yourself in the shoes of the court considering your argument and predict the court's reaction. Would the court nod its head approvingly or frown in disgust? For example, how would a court react to an argument that a fast food chain is responsible for the obesity of its patrons? Or that a prisoner who is denied access to video games is suffering cruel and unusual punishment?

A lawyer who advances silly, nonsensical, or ridiculous arguments will lose credibility with the court, her client, and opposing counsel. A lawyer must distinguish between a novel and creative argument using the law, and improbable, unrealistic arguments that have little hope of success because they have no basis in law or policy or common sense. Judging credibility comes with experience and practice, but lawyers must use common sense and judgment to decide which arguments are credible and which are not.

Practice Exercises

Complete the following exercises to reinforce your understanding of this chapter.

1. Define policy.
2. How do you identify policy in judicial opinions?
3. How do you identify policy in statutes?
4. List four uses of policy arguments.
5. How is society protected by the following requirements for a statutory marriage?
   a. Blood test for syphilis
   b. Obtaining a marriage license
   c. Waiting period between issuance of a license and the marriage ceremony
   d. Marriage ceremony attended by both the bride and groom and officiated by an authorized official
6. A court is considering whether a town's curfew for minors violates the minors' rights even if it protects them and the public. Of the five types of policy arguments discussed in this chapter, what type of policy argument could the town make?
7. A state's highest court recognized gay marriage in its jurisdiction. Of the five types of policy arguments discussed in this chapter, what type of policy argument could those opposed to gay marriage make?
8. A customer went into a convenience store to buy milk. A third party came into the store and while robbing the store, he shot the customer. Unbeknownst to the customer, the store had been frequently robbed, and the store owner could be found liable for negligent security. Of the five types of policy arguments discussed in this chapter, what type of policy argument could the victim make?
9. Courts in this jurisdiction have recognized a bystander may recover for negligent infliction of emotional distress. One element the plaintiff must prove is that she was "closely related" to the victim. The courts have defined "closely re-

lated" as parents, siblings, grandparents, or other relatives residing in the same residence.

A father witnessed the defendant shoot his daughter, the victim. The father had left the victim's mother when the victim was an infant. The father was going to the victim's house for the first time in ten years when he witnessed the shooting. The father now seeks to recover for the defendant's negligent infliction of emotional distress. Of the five types of policy arguments discussed in this chapter, what type of policy argument could the plaintiff-father and the defendant-shooter make?

10. Define judicial conservatism.
11. Name one reason why courts generally are conservative.
12. When drafting an argument that requires the court to expand the law, how can attorneys appeal to a court's conservative nature?
13. What does it mean when a court starts down a "slippery slope"?
14. Why is an argument based both on law and fairness stronger than an argument based on fairness alone?
15. A law legalized the use of marijuana for medicinal purposes. Courts interpreting this law have consistently ruled that it applies only to victims of terminal illnesses. A plaintiff has glaucoma, a non-fatal illness. The plaintiff seeks to use marijuana for medicinal purposes.

    Aware of the court's conservative nature, draft an argument that opposes an extension of the law.
16. Seller had a valid contract to deliver 100 widgets to Buyer's factory by 9:00 a.m. on January 8. Due to severe traffic on January 8, Seller arrived at Buyer's plant with the widgets at 9:22 a.m. Buyer refused to accept the widgets because Seller was late.

    Draft a fairness argument that supports Seller's position.
17. Ryan and Isabelle dated for two years before deciding to buy a house together. They equally contributed to purchase a house. Isabelle spent a lot of time carefully decorating and renovating the house. She bought all the furniture for the

house with her own money. A year later, Ryan and Isabelle broke up. Ryan and Isabelle both want the house. Each wants the other person to move out. The court must now resolve the issue.

Draft a fairness argument to present to the court on behalf of Isabelle.

Chapter 7

The Legal Argument: CREAC

OBJECTIVES

WHEN YOU FINISH READING THIS CHAPTER AND COMPLETE THE EXERCISES PROVIDED, YOU WILL BE ABLE TO

- UNDERSTAND HOW TO COMMUNICATE LEGAL ANALYSIS
- UNDERSTAND THE ROLE AND FUNCTION OF CREAC, AN ORGA-NIZATIONAL PARADIGM DESIGNED TO EXPRESS LEGAL ANALY-SIS IN WRITING

Legal analysis involves studying the law, synthesizing it in a coherent and holistic manner, and then applying it to your client's case while anticipating counterarguments. After analyzing a legal issue, lawyers communicate that analysis in writing in a way that is easy and obvious for the reader to understand. Good writing is a reflection of good analysis. Effective legal writing is clear, concise, and precise.

Lawyers typically analyze issues either objectively or persuasively. An objective analysis is unbiased and seeks to educate the reader about a legal issue or seeks to predict the likely legal outcome of an issue. A persuasive argument is biased and seeks to persuade the reader—usually a court or tribunal—about the merits of a client's legal position.

Lawyers present these arguments in a number of formats. An objective analysis is often written in an interoffice memorandum. An interoffice memorandum is an internal document that objectively summarizes the attorney's research and analysis regarding a client's legal issue and predicts an outcome. A persuasive argument is generally written in a memorandum of law or brief. A memorandum of law or brief is a persuasive document that an attorney submits to a court or other tribunal in support of a client's legal position.

Many legal writers employ organizational paradigms to clearly communicate their analysis in writing. These paradigms serve as a guide or template when drafting legal analyses. The paradigms include, but are not limited to: IRAC, CREAC, and CRAC. In each of these paradigms, each letter represents a specific component or building block of a legal argument. For example, the letters in IRAC represent: Issue, Rule(s), Application, and Conclusion. Although several variations exist, each paradigm functions similarly and aims to present the analysis of a legal issue clearly, concisely, and precisely.

While organizational paradigms are useful to novice legal writers, relying too heavily on paradigms without understanding how each component part builds on the next will weaken the sophistication of the written argument. Some students may be tempted to oversimplify the written expression of the analysis by treating the organizational paradigm as a prescribed formula. Instead, the argument ought to be viewed holistically. Once you understand how the paradigm is built and the purpose of each component part, you should be able to manipulate or even omit parts to fit the needs of the client, the complexity of the legal issue, the goals or needs of your legal problem, or the audience reviewing the document.

This chapter will explain one organizational paradigm, CREAC, and how it is used to express different forms of legal analysis, including analogical reasoning and rule-based reasoning. CREAC has five component parts, each building on the other. Each letter in CREAC represents a specific component part of the written expression of legal analysis: Conclusion, Rule, Explanation of the law, Application of the Law, and Conclusion. When drafted effectively, the parts combine in a cohesive, logical, and comprehensive expression of legal analysis. CREAC is a flexible paradigm that can be manipulated or translated to fit many different types of legal analyses or documents. The key is to understand how each component part of CREAC fits together.

A. CREAC Explained

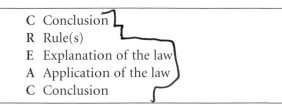

C Conclusion
R Rule(s)
E Explanation of the law
A Application of the law
C Conclusion

The following example illustrates the use of CREAC to analyze objectively a single issue using analogical or inductive reasoning. The issue is whether your client committed a trespass on the owner's land. The goal of this analysis is to predict whether your client's case has merit. Assume that you have already researched the applicable law in the controlling jurisdiction and analyzed your case under the law. Based on the nature of the case and the available authority, you decide to employ analogical reasoning to communicate your analysis.

Your Client's Legal Problem

Your client, the defendant, was sued for trespass. She suffers from seizures. While driving on a street that bordered the owner's land, your client had a seizure and lost control of her car. The car careened onto the owner's land, destroying his prized rose bushes.

1. The C in CREAC

Employing CREAC, organize the analysis of your client's legal issue by first stating your ultimate (C) conclusion regarding the particular issue discussed. This statement should be drafted in affirmative and precise language. If possible, include a brief statement of the reasoning that supports your conclusion. The CREAC paradigm requires a conclusion at the beginning of the argument because legal readers, such as lawyers and judges, expect to see the bottom line first. More importantly, legal readers can better understand the analysis when they know the conclusion at the outset. The conclusion provides the reader with the context to understand the analysis.

The C in Your Client's Case

The court will rule that the defendant did not trespass on the owner's land because she unintentionally entered the land.

2. The **R** in CREAC

Next, state the (R) rule(s) governing the issue. As discussed in chapter 2, rules are derived from case law or enacted law. Case rules can be either expressed or implied or synthesized from a variety of sources. For many legal issues, a number of rules may be applicable to fully analyze the client's case. When drafting the rules section, first state the general rule that governs the issue presented. A general rule is the comprehensive legal principle that is needed to resolve the issue. The general rule will provide the context of how the issue analyzed relates to the larger legal picture. For example, if a legal issue requires the analysis of three elements, the general rule will explain where the element analyzed fits within the larger issue. Then, if applicable, state more refined rules that are required to describe fully the general rule. In some situations, the general rule has terms that must be defined, or component parts that require sub-rules. State the rules in order of increasing levels of specificity. The rules section ought to resemble an inverted pyramid—the broadest rules at the top followed by increasingly specific rules until you reach the narrowest applicable rule. A well-drafted and complete R section will fully and concisely state all the law required to analyze a legal issue.

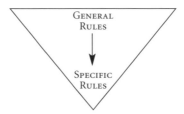

Rules frame the organization of the analysis. Rules drive the analysis. As such, CREAC requires lawyers to identify the rules after stating the conclusion. The reader now understands the issue, your overall conclusion, and the law or rules required to resolve the legal issue.

The R in Your Client's Case

Trespass to land prohibits the physical invasion of an unauthorized person onto another's private property. (General rule).[1] *An intention to trespass is not required, only an intention to enter the land. (Specific rule).*

3. The E in CREAC

Next, (E) explain the rules. This section of CREAC consists of a holistic discussion that educates or persuades the reader about how the precedent and other authoritative sources construe, apply, or interpret the rules. The E section explains the law and provides examples of how prior courts have resolved the same or similar issues even when the cases reach opposite results. This section could also include enacted law or secondary authority such as law review articles or legal treatises. The E section should reflect the full spectrum of authority required to explain the law.

The E section should educate the reader about the law. It may include a discussion of the critical facts in the relevant cases, the courts' holdings, and most importantly, the courts' reasoning. In some cases, an opinion will expressly state the reasoning. In other cases, however, the student must determine the court's implicit reasoning by analyzing the facts and holding of the relevant authority. The E section should include all the reasons that a court used to support its holding, including policy, to illustrate how a decision is consistent with the purposes behind the law.

If your analysis is supported in whole or part by an unexpressed or synthesized rule in the R section, the E section should explain how you arrived at or discovered the rule. Here, the E section would likely use cases or statutes to illustrate the unexpressed or synthesized rule. Because a court likely never articulated the rule,

---

1. Citations omitted throughout this example.

this section should establish how you determined the rule and provide a basis for a reader to judge its credibility.

The E section should not be a series of unconnected case briefs. Instead, this section should be organized around relevant themes or threads derived from the authority. Relevant themes or threads result from the synthesis of the applicable law. Think of this section as one holistic discussion that uses cases and other sources to explain or exemplify the law as opposed to a series of disconnected but related case annotations.

The purpose of the E section is to explain the relevant law. As such, this section should follow the R section.

The E in Your Client's Case

To determine a trespass, courts in Massachusetts examine whether the defendant's entry onto another's property was voluntary. For example, in <u>Samuels v. Philips</u>, the Massachusetts Appeals Court considered whether a defendant trespassed on another's property when the defendant entered the plaintiff's property by walking across an empty field. The defendant thought he was on public property. The court held that the defendant was liable for trespass because a person's intent to enter the land of another, not the person's intent to commit a trespass, satisfies the prima facie tort of trespass. The court reasoned that although the defendant did not intend to commit a trespass, he did intend to do the act which resulted in a trespass. In a later case, the appeals court in <u>Dunkin v. Ramy</u>, considered whether a defendant committed a trespass when he was pushed onto the property of another. The court held that the defendant was not liable because he did not intend the act that resulted in the trespass. In both cases, the court focused on the intent of the trespasser and examined how and not why the defendant entered the property of another. Both courts concluded that a defendant's intent to enter the land — not the intent to commit trespass — is determinative.

4. The A in CREAC

After describing the rules in the R section and explaining the rules in the E section, the A section applies the rules to the facts of your client's case. The rules stated in the R section and the themes developed in your E section should inform the A section. The R, E, and A sections should address parallel points and share the same thematic thread; the A section should follow logically from the R and E sections.

Rules → Explain Rules → Apply Rules to Facts

If you decide to employ analogical reasoning, the A section could include the four analytical steps described in chapter 3. First, state the point of your analysis. This statement is usually derived from the R and E sections and describes the analytical theme of your analysis. Second, state the fact-to-fact comparisons or distinctions between the determinative facts in your client's case and the determinative facts in the relevant case law. Under the inductive or analogical model, you must state how the facts of your client's case compare to the controlling (or persuasive) authorities. Under the inductive model, the similarities or distinctions between the facts of the cases will determine whether a court must follow the precedent. Third, explain the significance of the analogy. Simply describing the fact comparisons without explaining why that comparison is important is not legal analysis. Instead, point to the reasoning of the relevant case law to explain why your fact comparison determines the legal outcome. Fourth, state the conclusion.

The Four-part Argument

Step One: State the point of the analysis
Step Two: State the fact comparison
Step Three: Apply the court's reasoning
Step Four: Conclude

The E section and the A section are related but distinct parts of the analysis. The A section should not simply repeat the explanation of the law that you already discussed in the E section. Instead, compare the facts in the controlling authority first explained in the E section to the facts in your client's case. Explain the relationship between the facts of your client's case and the facts in the relevant authority—are they similar or different? If the facts are similar, then stare decisis applies and the outcome in your client's case ought to be similar to the outcomes of the relevant cases. Remember, legal analysis is like long division; you must show your work. Using the four-step approach will ensure a structured and thorough analysis of the issue.

The A in Your Client's Case

The defendant did not trespass because she involuntarily entered the owner's land. Like the defendant in <u>Dunkin</u>, who was pushed onto the property, the defendant in the present case involuntarily entered the owner's land when her seizure caused her car to enter another's property. Unlike the defendant in <u>Samuels</u>, who intended to enter the property, the defendant in the present case involuntarily entered the owner's land. A court will most likely follow the reasoning of <u>Dunkin</u> and <u>Samuels</u>, and similarly rule that the defendant's intent to do the act that resulted in the trespass and not the intent to trespass is required. Although the defendant knew she suffered from seizures and she intentionally drove her car, a court will likely focus on whether the trespass itself was intentional. Thus, a court will likely conclude that she is not liable because she never intended the act that resulted in the trespass.

5. The Final C in CREAC

The final Conclusion should concisely state the resolution of the issue analyzed. This statement should be brief and should never introduce new ideas. It reminds the reader of the bottom line.

The Final C in Your Client's Case

The defendant is not liable for trespass because she did not intend the act that resulted in the trespass. The defen-

dant's entrance onto the owner's land was caused by a seizure, an involuntary act.

B. The CREAC Argument: Inductive Analysis or Analogical Reasoning

Below, review the final written analysis of the client's case following the CREAC organizational paradigm using analogical reasoning.[2] Notice how each component of CREAC builds upon the former. When combined, the entire analysis represents a thorough and organized expression of the writer's analysis.

C   *The court will rule that the defendant did not trespass on the owner's land because she unintentionally entered the land. Trespass to land prohibits the physical invasion of*

R   *an unauthorized person onto another's private property. An intention to trespass is not required, only an intention to enter the land.*

E   *To determine a trespass, courts in Massachusetts examine whether the defendant's entry onto another's property was voluntary. For example, in Samuels v. Philips, the Massachusetts Appeals Court considered whether a defendant trespassed on another's property when the defendant entered the plaintiff's property by walking across an empty field. The defendant thought he was on public property. The court held that the defendant was liable for trespass because a person's intent to enter the land of another, not the person's intent to commit a trespass, satisfies the prima facie tort of trespass. The court reasoned that although the defendant did not intend to commit a trespass, he did intend to do the act which resulted in a trespass. In a later case, the appeals court in Dunkin v. Ramy, considered whether a defendant commits a trespass when he is pushed onto the property of another.*

---

2. Citations omitted in this example.

The court held that the defendant was not liable because he did not intend the act that resulted in the trespass. In both cases, the court focused on the intent of the trespasser and examined how and not why the defendant entered the property of another. Both courts concluded that a defendant's intent to enter the land—not the intent to commit trespass—is determinative.

A   The defendant did not trespass because she involuntarily entered the owner's land. Like the defendant in <u>Dunkin</u>, who was pushed onto the property, the defendant in the present case involuntarily entered the owner's land when her seizure caused her car to enter another's property. Unlike the defendant in <u>Samuels</u>, who intended to enter the property, the defendant in the present case involuntarily entered the owner's land. The court will most likely follow the reasoning of <u>Dunkin</u> and <u>Samuels</u>, and similarly rule that the defendant's intent to do the act that resulted in the trespass, and not the intent to trespass, is required. Although the defendant knew she suffered from seizures and she intentionally drove her car, the court will likely focus on whether the act of driving onto the property was intentional. Thus, the court will likely hold her not liable because
C   she never intended the act that resulted in the trespass. The defendant is not liable for trespass because she did not intend the act that resulted in the trespass. The defendant's entrance onto the owner's land was caused by a seizure, an involuntary act.

C. The CREAC Argument in a Multi-issue Problem

The example above illustrates the analysis of a single legal issue. CREAC, however, may also be used when a client's case involves more than one issue or when a single issue involves subparts. If your client's case requires the analysis of a multi-issue problem, then give the reader a roadmap or blueprint at the outset of the analysis in a holistic thesis paragraph. This introductory paragraph should give the reader the overall conclusion to the client's case, the general rule or rules required to analyze the case, and a brief summary of your analysis. Then use CREAC to organize the analysis of each issue or sub-issue.

For example, suppose your client would like you to determine whether his neighbor has a claim of adverse possession on a parcel of his land. The doctrine of adverse possession requires a showing that a party openly, continuously, exclusively, adversely, and notoriously possessed the land of another for a period of years. The issue may require the analysis of each element of adverse possession and a determination of whether the neighbor adversely possessed the property for the required time period. So, the organization of the analysis may look like this:

Thesis Paragraph

      C: Overall conclusion

      R: Rule of adverse possession

      A: Brief summary of the analysis

CREAC 1: Was neighbor's possession "open"?

CREAC 2: Was neighbor's possession "continuous"?

CREAC 3: Was neighbor's possession "exclusive"?

CREAC 4: Was neighbor's possession "adverse"?

CREAC 5: Was neighbor's possession "notorious"?

CREAC 6: Was neighbor's possession for the requisite time period?

In this example, the thesis paragraph states the overall conclusion—whether the neighbor did or did not adversely possess your client's property—sets the context of the problem, and offers the reader a concise roadmap of the issue. Then, each subpart of adverse possession is separately CREACed. In each of the six CREACs, the conclusion, rule, explanation, application, and conclusion are limited to the issue under consideration. For example, in CREAC 1 the analysis is limited only to whether neighbor's possession was "open." While rules in this CREAC might state that "open possession" is one element of adverse possession, the analysis is focused on the resolution of this one issue.

D. The CREAC Argument: Deductive Argument or Rule-based Reasoning

The example above demonstrates CREAC using analogical reasoning. This section will illustrate CREAC using rule-based reasoning. The first example below shows CREAC using deductive or rule-based reasoning structured around an expressed and unambiguous rule. The second example illustrates rule-based reasoning structured around an unexpressed rule. The third example illustrates rule-based reasoning using an ambiguous rule.

If you decide to employ rule-based reasoning, the analysis section should include the five analytical steps described in chapter 4. First, state the point of your analysis. Second, state the rule or rules applicable to the issue. Third, explain the rule. In some situations, after stating a rule it may not be necessary to explain the rule because the rule is clear, well-established, and unambiguous. In other situations, you may need to explain how you derived the rule — perhaps because a court fails to express the rule in its opinion or because a rule is synthesized from a variety of sources or because the rule is ambiguous and needs clarification. Fourth, apply the law to the facts. Fifth, state the conclusion.

The Five-part Argument: Rule-based Reasoning

Step One:	State the point of the analysis
Step Two:	State the rule
Step Three:	Explain the rule (if necessary)
Step Four:	Apply the law to the facts
Step Five:	Conclude

Recall from chapter 4 that when employing rule-based reasoning, the analysis section is structured around the rule itself and not fact comparisons. The idea is to apply the facts from your client's case to a stated proposition of law to deduce a conclusion.

1. The CREAC Argument: Rule-based Analysis Using an Expressed and Unambiguous Rule

In this example, the legal issue involves the application of an unambiguous statute to a set of facts. Earlier in this chapter, we noted that CREAC is a flexible paradigm and can be manipulated to meet the needs of the analysis. In this example, this analysis does not require an E section to explain the rule because the rule is clearly expressed and without ambiguity.[3]

> **Statute:** A person under the age of eighteen is not bound to a contract he enters.
>
> **The facts:** Your client is seventeen years old and entered a contract to buy a used car from his neighbor. The neighbor sues your client for breach of contract when your client fails to pay for the car.

C *The client is not liable for breach of contract because he is not bound by law to the contract. A person under*
R *the age of eighteen is not bound to a contract that the person enters. The client was seventeen years old when*
A *he entered the contract to purchase his neighbor's used car. The client is not liable for the breach because he is*
C *too young to be bound to the contract.*

Here, the analysis requires the application of facts to a stated legal proposition. The statute did not require an explanation—or E section—because the statute is clear and unequivocal. The writer could have chosen to include an E section to explain the derivation of the statute or the purpose of the law, but that explanation was not required to resolve the legal issue. Note the deductive nature of the analysis. The minor premise—the fact that the client is under eighteen years old—is applied to the major premise—the statute that voids contracts entered into by minors—to deduce a conclusion.

---

3. Citations omitted in this example.

2. The CREAC Argument: Rule-based Analysis for an Unexpressed Rule

In some situations, the court may not have clearly expressed a rule to resolve the case before it and no statute exists that speaks to the issue. A lawyer may need to infer or imply an unexpressed rule to resolve her client's case. Here, an E section is required to explain how the lawyer extrapolated the rule from the relevant cases. The idea is to establish the rule's credibility and veracity. Once the rule is explained, the lawyer simply applies the facts of the client's case to the rule to deduce a conclusion.

For example, assume that the state statutory code does not have a law on the books that voids contracts entered into by minors and no opinions expressly state a rule that governs the legal issue. Instead, the lawyer discovers an implied or unexpressed rule from the controlling cases. Here, merely stating the rule is not enough because the lawyer will need to show how she discovered the unexpressed rule from the cases. Once the rule is explained, the lawyer then applies the facts of the case to the rule to deduce a conclusion. Consider the following analysis[4]:

> **Unexpressed Rule:** A person under the age of eighteen is not bound to a contract he enters.
> **The facts:** Your client is seventeen years old and entered a contract to buy a used car from his neighbor. The neighbor sues your client for breach of contract when your client fails to pay for the car.
>
> C *The court will conclude that the client is not liable for breach of contract because he is not bound by law to the contract. A person under the age of eighteen is not*
> R *bound to a contract that he enters. In Smith v. Jones, the State Supreme Court considered whether a fifteen-year-old girl was bound to her contractual obligation to the*
> E *plaintiff to walk his dog. The court held that she was not*

---

4. Citations omitted in this example.

bound to the contract because her young age prevented her from fully understanding the rights and obligations of a contract. In a similar case, the Court of Appeals in Somol v. Taverna *considered whether an eighteen-year-old boy breached his contract with the plaintiff to mow his lawn. The court concluded that the defendant was contractually bound to cut the plaintiff's lawn because he was mature enough to understand the rights and obligations of a contractual relationship. Both cases imply that minors under age eighteen are unable to comprehend the nature of a contract and thus are not bound by them.*

A   *In the present case, the client is not bound to the contract he entered to purchase his neighbor's car. This jurisdiction voids contracts entered into by minors under the age of eighteen, because they lack the maturity necessary to understand fully the rights and obligations of a contractual relationship. The client was seventeen years old when he entered the contract. Thus, the client*

C   *is too young to be bound to the contract, and he is not liable for the breach.*

3. The CREAC Argument: Rule-based Analysis Using an Ambiguous or Vague Rule

In some legal problems, a rule is expressed but it is ambiguous or vague. Here, a lawyer would need to resolve the ambiguity before she can reach a conclusion. As discussed in chapter 5, enacted law is prone to ambiguous or vague language. To analyze an ambiguous or vague statutory provision, a lawyer must explain how the statutory language is resolved. Here, the analysis would require an E section to explain the rule. Once the statutory ambiguity is resolved, the lawyer applies the client's facts to the resolved statute to deduce a conclusion.

Suppose your client, the defendant, was charged with assault with a dangerous instrument. The prosecutor alleges that the defendant used a concrete sidewalk as a dangerous weapon when he smashed the victim's head against the sidewalk. The relevant state statute reads, "A person who assaults another with a gun, knife, or other dangerous instrument commits a class C felony." The statute is vague because it fails to define the categorical term "dangerous instrument." To analyze the issue, you must resolve the vague language to determine whether a concrete sidewalk qualifies as a dangerous instrument under the statute. In this example, a court in the controlling jurisdiction has not construed the statutory language. Consider the following analysis using CREAC[5]:

C   *A court will likely determine that the defendant did not commit an assault with a dangerous instrument because a concrete sidewalk is not designed to inflict harm. The relevant state statute reads, "A person who assaults*

R   *another with a gun, knife, or other dangerous instrument commits a class C felony." The legislature, however, failed to define the term "dangerous instrument." Despite this, a court will likely construe the term to include only instruments that are designed to inflict harm.*

E   *The meaning of the term "dangerous instruments" is not plain because it is a broad categorical term that could apply to almost any instrument. The legislative history of the statute, however, reveals that the legislature intended to include only objects that are designed to inflict harm or injury. Senator Amy Polk, the sponsor and drafter of the statute, stated during a Senate floor debate that "by passing this bill we protect our constituents from any criminal who uses a gun or a knife or anything else that was designed to kill or maim." Moreover, a court construing this statutory language will likely employ ejusdem generis, a tool of statutory construction that determines the breadth of a categorical term. In this statute, the phrase "dangerous instru-*

---

5. Citations omitted in this example.

ment" is preceded by the terms "gun" and "knife." Because a gun and a knife are designed specifically to inflict harm, a court would likely rule that the breadth of the term "dangerous instruments" is limited by these specific examples and conclude that the statute is limited instruments that are designed to inflict harm.

A   *In the present case, the defendant did not use a dangerous instrument during the assault. A concrete sidewalk is not designed to inflict harm but rather is designed to prevent harm by providing a stable and even walking*

C   *surface. As such, a court will likely determine that the defendant did not commit an assault with a dangerous instrument.*

The CREAC paradigm aids in the organization of legal analysis. It can be used with analogical reasoning or rule-based reasoning. The component parts of CREAC can and should be manipulated to best suit the analysis. If you understand the purpose behind each component part of CREAC, you can vary the paradigm to suit a wide variety of situations. Bear in mind that CREAC is simply an organizational tool. The strength and credibility of the analysis depends on the clarity of the written expression and the depth and sophistication of the analysis—not on the paradigm.

E. Fourteen Tips When Using CREAC

When using CREAC to communicate legal analysis, keep the following points in mind. These points address traps that often ensnare law students.

1. Analyze One Issue at a Time

Each CREAC ought to focus on a single legal issue. Do not analyze several issues at once. Focused analyses are easier for readers to digest and comprehend. If you have a multiple issue problem, then analyze each issue separately using CREAC, and provide the reader with a thesis paragraph at the outset of the analysis that ties the issue together and shows the big picture.

2. Conclude Only the Single Issue Analyzed

The C in each CREAC should conclude only as to the single issue analyzed. In some situations, an argument may consist of an analysis of multiple parts, requiring multiple CREACs. Each CREAC, however, ought to begin with a statement that offers a conclusion for the narrow part, element, or factor discussed and not the broader cause of action or legal principle. The broader conclusion is offered in the thesis paragraph at the outset of the analysis.

3. Offer All Rules Required to Analyze the Issue

In the R section of CREAC, offer all the rules required to resolve the issue. The R section could include enacted law, expressed rules, unexpressed or implied rules, and synthesized rules. Be sure to structure this section beginning with the broadest rule and then offer rules of increasing specificity. Remember that definitions are rules.

4. Explain the Law before Applying the Law

Before applying the law to the facts of your case, explain the law if needed. Then, you can refer to that law when applying it to your client's case. Discussing the law when you are applying that law to your client's facts can confuse and overwhelm the reader. The reader first has to comprehend the law before she can understand how that law applies to your case. For example, when employing analogical reasoning, describe the critical facts of the controlling cases in the E section before comparing and/or contrasting those facts to the critical facts in your client's case in the A section.

When drafting the E section, avoid a superficial explanation of the law; instead, explain the law thoroughly. Be sure to offer the key facts, reasoning, and holdings of the relevant cases. Be sure to include all relevant authority and not just authority that benefits your client's positions. Deal with negative authority. Do not ignore or omit it. Also, avoid "brief stacking" by simply offering a series of case annotations or briefs in the E section. Instead, explain the law using the common themes or threads that you identified in the authority. Synthesize similar cases and explain how the law developed, changed, broadened, or narrowed over time.

5. In the "A" Section, Start with the Point of the Argument

In either analogical or rule-based reasoning, start the A section by stating the point of the argument. Akin to a topic sentence, this point statement orients the reader to the key aspect of the analysis and how the law applies to the client.

6. For Inductive-type Arguments That Compare Facts:

a. State the Fact-to-Fact Analogy

Whenever possible, refer to a determinative fact in the precedent when comparing that fact to a fact in your client's case. Don't merely mention the precedent without showing which facts in the precedent are comparable to the facts in your client's case. Don't make the reader refer back to an explanation of a case to see how the facts in that case apply to your client's case. The reader should never have to work to follow your analysis.

> **Ineffective:** Like the defendant in *Jones*, our client also has an alibi because he was home during the alleged crime.
> **Effective:** Like the defendant in *Jones*, who had an alibi because he was in a movie theater during that alleged crime, our client also has an alibi because he was at home during the alleged crime.

b. Prove the Significance of the Analogy

After stating a fact analogy or distinction, explain why that fact comparison is important. Simply pointing to a fact comparison without explaining why the comparison is important is not legal analysis. Instead, remind the reader why the fact comparison suggests a legal result.

> **Ineffective:** The defendant in the present case is not guilty of the crime charged because he has a credible alibi. Like the defendant in *Jones*, who proved that he had an alibi because he was in a movie theater during that crime, the defendant in the present case also has an alibi because he was home during the crime. Therefore, the defendant is not guilty.
>
> **Effective:** The defendant in the present case is not guilty of the crime charged because he has a credible alibi. Like the defendant in *Jones*, who proved that he had an alibi because he was in a movie theater during that crime, the defendant in the present case also has an alibi because he was home during the crime. The court will follow the reasoning of *Jones* and rule that defendants who establish sufficient evidence of an alibi cannot be found guilty of the crime. In the present case, the defendant is not guilty because he establishes credible evidence of an alibi.

7. For Deductive-type Arguments Consider the Syllogism

A syllogism is a three-part argument that requires a major premise, a minor premise, and a conclusion. The major premise is the law. The minor premise is the facts in a client's case. The conclusion is the application of the law to the facts. Instead of comparing facts, consider a deductive-type argument by applying the client's facts to the law to deduce a conclusion.

> **Effective:** A defendant who establishes a credible alibi cannot be guilty of the crime charged. The defendant in the

present case proved that he was home during the crime. The defendant is not guilty of the crime charged because he has a credible alibi.

8. Don't Be Conclusory

Instead of merely stating the legal conclusion, explain how you reached that conclusion. Sometimes, after immersing themselves in a legal problem, students lose perspective and assume that the reader is already acquainted with the law and analysis. To avoid this, explain each step of the analysis. Don't assume the reader will understand your argument without a clear and logical development of the analysis. Like giving someone directions to your house, explain each small step so your reader won't get lost.

9. Don't Fight the Law or Your Client's Facts

It is unethical to omit unfavorable authority or facts or bend the law or distort facts to fit the conclusion you desire. Instead, deal with the law and facts head-on and embrace any ambiguity, inconsistency, negative authority, or damaging facts.

10. Avoid the Stretch Argument

Legally tenuous or far-fetched arguments will likely fail and undermine your credibility. Sound, logical, and credible arguments are always more persuasive than unrealistic or implausible arguments.

11. Remember the Alternative Argument

Cover all your bases. Consider including an alternative argument to your argument-in-chief. Offering more than one legal route to prevail increases a lawyer's chances of success. If a court does not agree or is not persuaded by one argument, it could still be persuaded by an alternative argument.

12. Anticipate and Analyze the Opponent's Argument

Don't ignore opposing arguments. Ignoring them won't make them go away. Deal with the weaknesses in your case directly. In objective legal writing, the opponent's position might be the winning position. In persuasive legal writing, address the other side's likely arguments by refuting them or explaining why they lack merit. Deal with any weaknesses in your case by anticipating counterarguments.

13. Organize the Analysis around a Common Theme

A well-drafted CREAC will have a common theme or thread. Each component part of the paradigm will reinforce that theme. The first **C** will introduce the theme; the **R** and the **E** sections will state, explain, and illustrate the theme; and the **A** section will analyze arguments under that same theme. A thematic argument reinforces the key point or points in every part of CREAC. A CREAC that lacks a common theme will appear fractured and disconnected.

14. Be Flexible

Think about the purpose behind each component part of CREAC. Once you develop a fluid understanding of CREAC, you will be able to apply it in different contexts and in a variety of ways. CREAC is a starting point and should be adapted to meet the simplicity or complexity of each legal problem. For example, you may not need an **E** section if the rule is clear and unequivocal. In other situations, you may not need an **A** section if the point of the analysis is to determine what law applies or what law a court should adopt—not to apply a set of facts to the law. Think of CREAC as a flexible and mutable paradigm instead of a rigid formula.

Practice Exercises

Complete the following exercises to reinforce your understanding of this chapter.

1. What are some differences and similarities between CREAC and IRAC?
2. When would a writer vary the component parts of CREAC?
3. Answer the following questions:
   a. What do the letters of CREAC represent?
   b. What is the purpose of the E?
   c. What is the purpose of the A?
4. Why is it important to state the conclusion first in an argument?
5. The following sentences are from an argument. Unscramble the sentences and put them in a logical order following CREAC.
   a. *Voluntary manslaughter is the unlawful killing of another without malice, but with adequate provocation. Utopia Gen. Law § 52 (2007).*
   b. *Like the defendant in State v. Z, who was adequately provoked when he found his wife in bed with another, the defendant in the present case was also adequately provoked when he was cut off by a speeding motorist on a crowded highway. In the heat of passion, with no time to reflect on the consequences of his actions, the defendant in the present case, like the defendant in State v. Z, committed voluntary manslaughter. In the present case, the defendant, after being cut off by a speeding motorist, pulled a hand gun from his glove compartment, and shot the speeding driver.*
   c. *The defendant in the present case is guilty of voluntary manslaughter because he killed another in the heat of passion.*
   d. *The present court will follow the reasoning of the court in State v. Z, where the court reasoned that killings that result from adequate provocation, or in the heat of passion,*

are voluntary manslaughters. The court will find that the defendant committed voluntary manslaughter.

e. *Adequate provocation depends on whether a defendant was reasonably provoked to kill another. For example, in State v. Z, the defendant found his wife in bed with another. Consumed with rage, the defendant grabbed a shotgun and killed the victim. The court in State v. Z held that the defendant was guilty of voluntary manslaughter because he killed another in the heat of passion. The court in State v. Z reasoned that the defendant committed voluntary manslaughter because he was reasonably provoked and reacted without time to reflect on his actions.*

Conclusion

Legal analysis is a skill, unique to the legal profession. A well-analyzed legal issue is the result of careful thinking, critical reading, and experience. Mastering legal analysis is attainable by understanding the basic principles discussed in this book. By providing an introduction and foundation to legal analysis, we hope this book helps you understand *legal analysis—the fundamental skill.*

Glossary of Terms

Ambiguous term. A term in a statute that has more than one meaning.

Analogical analysis. A strategy of legal analysis that compares facts in cases or the characteristic of facts in cases to the facts of a client's case.

Analogy. An inference that if two or more facts or characteristics are similar in one respect, they will be similar in other respects.

Appellate court. A court that reviews errors of law, fact, or procedure made in a prior court's determination of the same case.

Attorney. A person admitted in a jurisdiction to practice law.

Authority. Any legal source used by courts and attorneys to oppose or support a legal proposition.

Avoid surplusage. A maxim of statutory construction that presumes that every word in a statute is meaningful and that a legislature would not enact law with surplus or redundant terms.

Balancing test. A legal test that consists of several factors that courts weigh to reach a conclusion.

Bill. A draft of a proposed law introduced by a legislator.

Binding authority. Law that a court must follow.

Broad analogy. An analogy that draws general fact comparisons that relate to but are not necessarily parallel to the critical facts of the precedent.

Case. A judicial proceeding that determines a controversy between two or more parties.

Case-at-bar. A cause of action currently before a court.

Case law. Law derived from the judiciary.

Case of first impression. A case that raises an issue not yet resolved by the court, and thus no precedent exists.

Case synthesis. A process that combines several opinions in order to identify a common denominator among the precedents.

Certification. A procedure authorized by state law that refers a state issue originally brought in federal court to that state's highest court of appeals.

Common law. The rules and legal principles derived from judicial decisions, judgments, and decrees, rendered in the absence of enacted law.

Concurring opinion. A separate opinion that agrees with the result of the majority opinion but for different reasons.

Constitutional questions. A maxim of statutory construction that requires a court to avoid an interpretation of a statute that raises a constitutional question.

Court. A branch of government that interprets the law and resolves legal disputes.

Court brief. A persuasive memorandum of law that attorneys submit to a court in support of their client's legal position. (Do not confuse this with students' case briefs).

CREAC. An organizational formula for legal writing that represents: Conclusion, Rule(s), Explanation of the law, Application of the law, and Conclusion.

Critical facts. Facts from the controlling precedent that a court found dispositive when it resolved a legal dispute.

Decision. The judicial determination of a dispute.

Deductive reasoning. A strategy of legal analysis that deduces a conclusion by applying facts to a stated legal premise.

Dictum (dicta). The part of a court's opinion that does not relate to the resolution of the case.

Disposition. The component of an opinion that resolves a legal matter.

Dissenting opinion. A separate opinion that disagrees with the majority's holding.

Distinction. A contrast between the critical facts of a precedent and the facts in a case-at-bar.

Economic arguments. A policy argument that focuses on financial considerations, such as the allocation of judicial resources.

Ejusdem generis. ("Of the same kind.") A maxim of statutory construction that requires courts to construe a general word in a statute that follows a list of specific words to include only things of the same type specified in the list.

Element. A component part of a legal test that must be satisfied or met.

Enacted law. Law derived from a legislature.

Expressed rule. A clearly expressed legal principle found in a judicial opinion.

Expressio unius est exclusio alterius. ("The expression of one excludes the other.") When a statute includes a list of terms, this maxim of statutory construction prevents a court from adding any additional terms.

Extrapolation. A process of identifying a common characteristic among several facts by abstracting more general characteristics from specific traits.

Factor. A component part of a legal test that the court may consider. Every factor need not weigh in favor of a party to satisfy a test.

Facts. The events, circumstances, or objects stated in an opinion that relate to the ultimate resolution of the matter.

Fairness. A court's considerations of equity, impartiality, and justness, when deciding legal issues.

Fairness and justice arguments. Type of policy argument that considers whether a judicial disposition is impartial and honest with respect to all parties and is free from bias or favoritism.

Hierarchy. Different levels of courts within a jurisdiction.

Highest court of appeal. The highest level appellate court within a jurisdiction.

Holding. The component of an opinion that resolves the question(s) presented to the court.

Implied rule. A rule that is not articulated in the body of an opinion.

Inductive reasoning. A strategy of analysis that allows a lawyer to induce a conclusion by establishing a legal analogy between the key facts in the controlling cases and the facts in the client's case.

In pari materia. ("On like subject matter.") A maxim of statutory construction that requires courts to read statutes on the same subject matter consistently with each other.

Institutional competence arguments. Policy arguments that focus on whether the legislature or the courts are better suited to resolve a legal issue.

Intermediate court of appeals. An appellate court that reviews errors of law from a trial court in jurisdictions that have a three-level court hierarchy.

Interoffice memorandum. An internal legal document that summarizes an attorney's research and analysis and that objectively predicts a court's decision regarding specific legal issues.

IRAC. An organizational formula for legal writing, that represents: Issue, Rule(s), Application of the law, and Conclusion.

Issue. The component of an opinion that presents the legal question that the court is asked to resolve.

Judge. A person who presides over legal disputes and decides controversies between parties.

Judgment. A court's final determination of a dispute that resolves the rights and liabilities of parties in a lawsuit.

Judicial administration policy arguments. Policy arguments that focus on the importance of an efficient and fair judicial system.

Judicial conservatism. A court's inherent reluctance to change the law.

Jurisdiction. The power of a court to decide a case or controversy.

Law. Rules which govern persons and entities rights, duties, obligations, and liabilities.

Lawyer. A person licensed to practice law.

Legal analogy. An inference that if the determinative facts in the controlling authority are similar to the determinative facts in the client's case, then the holdings or legal conclusions ought to be similar.

Legal analysis. Strategies lawyers employ to determine, predict, or persuade legal outcomes of cases.

Legal test. A judicial inquiry that determines whether a rule has been satisfied.

Legislative history. The paper trail of a bill as it works its way through the different stages of the legislative process.

Legislative intent. The reasons behind the enactment of a statute.

Legislature. The branch of government that enacts laws.

Lenity. A maxim of statutory construction that requires a court to resolve an ambiguity in a criminal statute in favor of the accused.

Major premise. The major premise is the first premise in a syllogism and usually describes a quality, character, property, or attribute that is true to all members of a class.

Minor premise. The minor premise is the second premise in a syllogism that describes some characteristic of a member of the class within the major premise.

Maxim of statutory construction. A generally recognized guide or custom that a court may use to interpret statutory ambiguity.

Memorandum of law. A document summarizing a lawyer's research and analysis.

Narrow analogy. An legal analogy that draws specific fact comparisons between the case-at-bar and the precedent.

Normative arguments. Policy arguments that focus on social utility, such as security, public safety, or public health concerns.

Noscitur a sociis. ("It is known from its associates."). A maxim of statutory construction that requires a court to construe an ambiguous term by looking at its neighboring terms for guidance.

On point. A controlling case that is dispositive of the legal issue in a client's case.

Opinion. Written statement of a court explaining how it reached its decision.

Persuasive authority. Law that a court is not bound to follow, such as a case from another jurisdiction.

Persuasive brief. A formal written document submitted to a court to convince it to resolve an issue in a particular way.

Plain meaning doctrine. A rule of statutory construction that requires courts to use the ordinary and plain meaning of terms found in a statute.

Point sentence. A topic sentence that introduces the point of an analysis.

Policy. The purpose behind a law. The reason why a legislature or courts made a law.

Precedent. A judicial decision or opinion that serves as an example of how a subsequent court can resolve a similar question of law under a similar set of facts.

Presumption of internal consistency. A maxim of statutory construction that requires a court to interpret a statute to promote consistency within the statute.

Prima facie **case.** A case that alleges sufficient evidence on its face.

Primary authority. A source of authority that represents the law.

Procedural history. The component of an opinion that traces the case as it worked its way through the court system.

Reasoning. The component of an opinion that explains how the court reached its decision.

Remedial statutes canon. A maxim of statutory construction that requires courts to construe broadly an ambiguous statute until the statute's remedial purpose is accomplished.

Rule. A principle of law employed or adopted to resolve a legal issue. A legal principle set by an authoritative body prohibiting or requiring action or forbearance.

Rule-based reasoning. A mode of legal analysis that requires a lawyer to apply a set of facts to a stated legal premise, like a statute or common-law rule.

Rule synthesis. A process that blends relevant cases to develop a holistic rule that incorporates the holdings of the applicable cases.

Secondary authority. A source of authority that consists of any relevant source, other than the law. It is persuasive, never binding, on a court.

Slippery slope. A judicial determination that results in unclear limits of liability, potentially increasing the number of lawsuits.

Stare decisis. A principle that requires courts to follow precedent when deciding similar cases.

Statute. An act of a legislature that, among other things, proscribes and governs conduct. It is a formal written enactment of a legislature.

Statutory construction. A judicial analysis that interprets ambiguous or vague terms in statutes.

Syllogism. A logical model that has a major premise, a minor premise, and a conclusion.

Titles are not controlling. A maxim of statutory construction prevents courts from using a statute's title to resolve statutory ambiguity.

Totality of the circumstances test. A test that requires the court to consider all of the circumstances relevant to the case.

Trial court. A court where evidence is first introduced and considered.

Vague term. A term in a statute that has no defined limits.

Index